U.S. Department of Justice
Office of Justice Programs
810 Seventh Street N.W.
Washington, DC 20531

Janet Reno
Attorney General
U.S. Department of Justice

Raymond C. Fisher
Associate Attorney General

Laurie Robinson
Assistant Attorney General

Noël Brennan
Deputy Assistant Attorney General

Jeremy Travis
Director, National Institute of Justice

Office of Justice Programs	National Institute of Justice
World Wide Web Site	World Wide Web Site
http://www.ojp.usdoj.gov	*http://www.ojp.usdoj.gov/nij*

Legal Interventions in Family Violence: Research Findings and Policy Implications

A Project of the American Bar Association's Criminal Justice Section, Commission on Domestic Violence, Center on Children and the Law, and Commission on Legal Problems of the Elderly presented to the National Institute of Justice.

July 1998
NCJ 171666

Jeremy Travis
Director

Bernard Auchter
*Program Manager, Violence Against Women and
Family Violence Research and Evaluation Program*

John Thomas
Program Manager, Research in Action Partnerships

Criminal Justice Section
Thomas C. Smith, Director
Project Staff
Susan W. Hillenbrand, Project Director
Barbara E. Smith, Research Investigator
Laura Nickles, Research Associate

Center on Children and the Law
Howard A. Davidson, Director
Project Advisor
Howard A. Davidson

Commission on Domestic Violence
Roberta Valente, Director
Project Advisors
Roberta Valente
Deborah Goelman

Commission on Legal Problems of the Elderly
Nancy Coleman, Director
Project Advisor
Lori Stiegel

The views expressed herein have not been approved by the House of Delegates or the Board of Governors of the American Bar Association and, accordingly, they should not be construed as representing the policy of the American Bar Association. Further, this publication has not been endorsed by the American Bar Association entities involved in its production, including the Section of Criminal Justice, Commission on Domestic Violence, Center on Children and the Law, and Commission on Legal Problems of the Elderly.

This program was supported under award number 96–IJ–CX–K002 to the American Bar Association by the National Institute of Justice, Office of Justice Programs, U.S. Department of Justice. Findings and conclusions of the research reported here are those of the authors and do not necessarily reflect the official position or policies of the U.S. Department of Justice.

The National Institute of Justice is a component of the Office of Justice Programs, which also includes the Bureau of Justice Assistance, the Bureau of Justice Statistics, the Office of Juvenile Justice and Delinquency Prevention, and the Office for Victims of Crime.

Table of Contents

Message From The Director vi

Introduction vii

About This Publication viii

Chapter One: Research on Legal Interventions in Child Maltreatment Cases 1

   Children's Testimony 3

      The Emotional Effects of Testifying on Sexually Abused Children 3
      Debra Whitcomb, Gail S. Goodman, Desmond K. Runyan, and Shirley Hoak

      Techniques for Improving Children's Testimony 4
      Debra Whitcomb

      Effects of Cognitive Interviewing and Practice on Children's Recall Performance . 7
      Karen J. Saywitz, R. Edward Geiselman, and Gail K. Bornstein

      **The Use of Closed-Circuit Television and Videotaped Testimony in
      Child Sexual Abuse Trials: An Evaluation of BJA's Funding Program** 8
      Sharon G. Elstein, Barbara E. Smith, Howard Davidson, Donald Rebovich,
      Kathy Free, Mark Ells, and Caren Sempel

      **Children's Testimony and Their Perceptions
      of Stress in and out of the Courtroom** 10
      Karen J. Saywitz and Rebecca Nathanson

   Prosecution of Child Abuse and Neglect Cases 12

      The Prosecution of Child Sexual and Physical Abuse Cases 12
      Barbara E. Smith and Sharon Goretsky Elstein

      Prosecuting Child Physical Abuse Cases: A Case Study in San Diego 14
      Barbara E. Smith

      Justice System Processing of Child Abuse and Neglect Cases 15
      Noy S. Davis and Susan J. Wells

      **Coordinating Criminal and Juvenile Court Proceedings in
      Child Maltreatment Cases** 17
      Debra Whitcomb and Mark Hardin

   Sentencing 20

      **The Probation Response to Child Sexual Abuse Offenders:
      How Is it Working?** 20
      Barbara E. Smith, Susan W. Hillenbrand, and Sharon R. Goretsky

      **Managing Adult Sex Offenders in the Community—A Containment
      Approach** 23
      Kim English, Suzanne Pullen, and Linda Jones

Impact of Domestic Violence on Children's Behavior ... 25

Children of Battered Women: The Relation of Child Behavior to Family Violence and Maternal Stress ... 25
David A. Wolfe, Peter Jaffe, Susan Kaye Wilson, and Lydia Zak

Other ... 27

Parental Drug Testing in Child Abuse and Neglect Cases: The Washington, D.C., Experience ... 27
Lisa C. Newmark

Chapter Two: Research on Legal Interventions in Elder Abuse Cases ... 29

Coordination and Collaboration ... 30

Working Relationships Between Adult Protective Services, Aging Agencies, and Law Enforcement Agencies—A Short-Term Project ... 30
Toshio Tatara and Margaret Rittman

Collaboration Between Protective Services and Law Enforcement: The Massachusetts Model ... 31
Donna M. Reulbach and Jane Tewksbury

Recommendations to State Courts ... 34

Recommended Guidelines for State Courts Handling Cases Involving Elder Abuse ... 34
Lori A. Stiegel

Chapter Three: Research on Legal Interventions in Domestic Violence Cases ... 37

Batterer and Victim Characteristics ... 39

Findings About Partner Violence From the Dunedin Multidisciplinary Health and Development Study ... 39
Terrie E. Moffitt, Avshalom Caspi, and Phil A. Silva

Florida Mortality Review Project: Executive Summary ... 40
Byron Johnson, De Li, and Neil Websdale

Civil Protection Orders ... 43

Civil Protection Orders: Legislation, Current Court Practice, and Enforcement ... 43
Peter Finn and Sarah Colson

The Effectiveness of Civil Protection Orders ... 47
Susan Keilitz, Paula Hannaford, and Hillery S. Efkeman

Effects of Restraining Orders on Domestic Violence Victims ... 49
Adele Harrell and Barbara Smith

Re-abuse in a Population of Court-Restrained Male Batterers: Why Restraining Orders Don't Work ... 52
Andrew R. Klein

Arrest ... 54

Does Arrest Deter Domestic Violence? ... 54
Janell D. Schmidt and Lawrence W. Sherman

Must We Stop Arresting Batterers?: Analysis and Policy Implications of New Police Domestic Violence Studies ... 55
Joan Zorza

Mandatory Arrest of Batterers: A Reply to Its Critics ... 57
Evan Stark

Determining Police Response to Domestic Violence Victims ... 58
Eve S. Buzawa and Thomas Austin

Prosecution and Defense ... 59

Prosecution Response to Domestic Violence: Results of a Survey of Large Jurisdictions ... 59
Donald J. Rebovich

The Indianapolis Domestic Violence Prosecution Experiment ... 62
David A. Ford and Mary Jean Regoli

Validity of "Battered Woman Syndrome" in Criminal Cases Involving Battered Women ... 64
Malcolm Gordon

Impact of Evidence Concerning Battering and Its Effects in Criminal Trials Involving Battered Women ... 66
Mary Ann Dutton

Trend Analysis: Expert Testimony on Battering and its Effects in Criminal Cases ... 68
Janet Parrish

Prosecuting Domestic Violence Cases With Reluctant Victims: Assessing Two Novel Approaches in Milwaukee ... 71
Robert C. Davis, Barbara E. Smith, and Laura Nickles

Court-Ordered Treatment ... 73

The Impact of Court-Ordered Treatment for Domestic Violence Offenders ... 73
Adele Harrell

The Role of Drug and Alcohol Abuse in Domestic Violence and Its Treatment: Dade County's Domestic Violence Court Experiment ... 74
John S. Goldkamp, with Doris Weiland, Mark Collins and Michael White

Other ... 76

Corporate Sector Response to Domestic Violence ... 76
Nancy E. Isaac

Statistical Reports on Family Violence ... 78

Message From the Director

Recent research has shed considerable light on family violence and various efforts to combat it within the justice system. Much of the research has direct, practical application for prosecutors, judges, defense attorneys, victim/witness advocates, and members of the law enforcement community. Typically, however, these practitioners are so caught up in trying to meet the day-to-day demands of an overburdened system that they cannot accord family violence research the attention it deserves.

The National Institute of Justice and the American Bar Association share a similar mission: to inform our constituencies about the effectiveness of practical responses to family violence. This publication, the product of a research partnership, is intended to provide busy practitioners with a "quick and easy" overview of the wide range of available research on family violence and to highlight a few major studies and their practical implications. The goal is to encourage practitioners to "think research" in dealing with family violence.

NIJ is optimistic that the continuing research in this area can improve criminal justice responses to family violence by making practitioners aware of what works in which types of situations. It is our hope that this publication will serve that purpose.

Jeremy Travis
Director, National Institute of Justice

Introduction

Violence inflicted by one family member against another includes child physical and sexual abuse and neglect; domestic violence; and elder abuse. Sorting out and understanding violent behavior among family members presents complex challenges. Many factors render traditional criminal justice responses inappropriate or ineffective—the cyclical nature of family violence, the relationship between the perpetrator and victim, the causes and effects for both perpetrator and victim; the frequent ambivalence of the victim/witnesses toward involvement of the criminal justice system because of coercion by or fear of the perpetrator, and the guarded privacy traditionally accorded the family.

As public awareness and concern about family violence have increased in recent years, many practitioners have sought to fashion responses that take into account the needs of victims as well as punishment and treatment of perpetrators. However, the myriad variables surrounding these responses often send complex and sometimes conflicting signals to even the most sophisticated criminal justice practitioners. Research performs an invaluable function by identifying and sorting through these variables to determine how they affect, and are affected by, various criminal justice responses.

About This Publication

This publication contains "bottom line" information from articles written by researchers about their own work or in several instances about other researchers' work on subjects of immediate concern to practitioners: collaborative efforts between police and protection agencies, arrest policies, protection orders, battered women defense strategies, sentencing, batterer treatment, child sexual abuse, and children's testimony.

The research findings are the core of the document. It is from these that the researchers have derived their implications for practice and it is from these that the reader may derive additional—and perhaps different—implications for their own particular practice.

The studies summarized in this publication represent only those that relate specifically to how the criminal justice system addresses family violence. Other aspects of family violence, such as those associated with custody and divorce proceedings are not included. Also not included are findings from ongoing research mandated by the groundbreaking Violence Against Women Act of 1994—for example, the effects of the "full faith and credit" clause as it pertains to protection orders.

Most of the articles were written by the researchers who conducted the studies, but several were written by commentators on research undertaken by others.

The summaries were compiled and edited by staff of the ABA dissemination project who have generally maintained the language and terms from the original documents even when aware of their limitations.

In most instances the summaries merely mirror major findings and implications in the underlying documents. When project staff have drawn practical implications from the findings, this is noted in the text. All the research highlighted here has received scrutiny, either through peer review or review by funding agencies or publishers.

As science investigates complex, sensitive, and private issues, such as family violence, various methodological limitations can cloud the interpretation of findings. Reported results can vary depending on the type of sampled population; specific variables measured; and other personal, family, or community characteristics not included in the research effort. For example, secondary analysis and replication efforts arising from the seminal 1984 Minneapolis Domestic Violence Experiment have yielded differing results regarding the extent to which mandatory arrest and "no drop" prosecution policies prevent further violence.

The long-range aim of this publication is to encourage continued investigation into family violence and continued critical review of the results so that practitioners can make better informed decisions about practical criminal justice responses.

Chapter One: Research on Legal Interventions in Child Maltreatment Cases

During the past decade, there has been a proliferation of research on child abuse, especially child sexual abuse. While many of the research findings relate to legal interventions to assist child victims in the civil arena, the 13 research projects summarized in this chapter were selected because of their relevance for criminal justice practitioners. These are organized into four main research topics: children's testimony, prosecution of child abuse and neglect cases, sentencing, and the impact of domestic violence on children. The findings can help law enforcement officers, prosecutors, victim/witness advocates, probation officers, and judges better respond to these especially vulnerable victims and their families.

Children's Testimony

Researchers and practitioners have questioned the impacts, positive and negative, of children testifying in court cases and have searched for ways to make the process less onerous for children while protecting the rights of the accused. Five research studies are summarized; four center on testimony in child sexual abuse cases and the fifth one on children's testimony in general.

The first study examines whether appearing in court benefits or harms sexually abused children. It concludes that testifying can be both harmful and beneficial depending upon the circumstances under which, and the number of times, children testify. Children are less stressed when there is a high level of maternal support and when the environment is child friendly. The second study looks at interviewing, communication enhancement, and courtroom preparation techniques and offers suggestions to improve the way professionals interview children. The third examines the effects of cognitive interviewing techniques and concludes that these techniques can help children's recall. The fourth is an evaluation of the Bureau of Justice Assistance's (BJA's) closed-circuit television and videotaped testimony funding program, which contains suggestions for criminal justice planners and professionals interested in starting or expanding their use of closed-circuit television or videotape technologies. The last summary is of a research project that explores the impact of the courtroom environment on the quality of evidence given by children and the level of system-induced stress on children. It concludes that testifying in a child-friendly environment yields more accurate testimony and results in less stress to the child.

Prosecution of Child Abuse and Neglect Cases

Prosecution of child sexual and physical abuse and child neglect cases presents special challenges for prosecutors and victim/witness advocates. Much has been learned in the past decade about how to meet those challenges and effectively prosecute cases while protecting the child and the rights of the accused.

The first of the two studies summarized on this topic examines the outcomes of nearly 1,000 child sexual abuse cases in 10 counties, including case dynamics, the use of specialized techniques, case dispositions, and sentences imposed. Implications drawn from the study results offer suggestions to improve the response of the criminal justice system to such cases. The focus of the second summary is a case study of San Diego's multiagency response to child physical abuse cases that contains suggestions to help other communities successfully prosecute these types of cases.

Sentencing

Probation is a common or even primary sentence for persons convicted of child sexual abuse. Most probation orders require the offender to seek treatment and stay away from the victim and/or other children. Two research studies are included. The first study examines the use of probation as an alternative to incarceration, or in conjunction with incarceration, in child sexual abuse cases. The results are based on a national survey on probation departments' supervision of child sexual abuse offenders and case studies in four jurisdictions that explored the effectiveness of probation in these types of cases. The summary contains recommendations for improving the response to these offenders. The second study also looks at the management of adult sex offenders but is broader as it includes both probation and parole departments and it deals with adult sex offenders whose victims are adults as well as children. It is included because the findings apply to those who sexually offend against children and many of the findings and recommendations mirror those of the first study.

Impact of Domestic Violence on Children's Behavior

Children who witness domestic violence often suffer psychological and behavior problems. The article included here measures the extent of difficulties experienced by children of domestic violence. It concludes that children from violent homes experience significantly more behavior problems than those from nonviolent homes. This is especially true for boys, for children exposed to a higher frequency and intensity of physical violence, and for children whose mothers report more negative life events.

Children's Testimony

Selected Findings and Implications Drawn From

The Emotional Effects of Testifying on Sexually Abused Children

by Debra Whitcomb, Gail S. Goodman, Desmond K. Runyan, and Shirley Hoak[1]

Purpose of Research

To examine whether testifying in court benefits or harms sexually abused children.

Methods

Three studies that used the same research instruments to measure mental health were analyzed:

- A National Institute of Justice (NIJ)-funded study in North Carolina that reassessed the mental health of 62 children between the ages of 6 and 17 (an earlier grant from the National Center on Child Abuse and Neglect had assessed their mental health 5 months after referral to the study). Reports of sexual abuse of all of the children had been substantiated by child protection agencies.

- An NIJ-funded study in Denver that assessed the mental health of children between the ages of 4 and 17. All of the children's perpetrators were charged in criminal courts in three counties in the Denver area. The children's mental health was evaluated four times: at the time they were referred to the study, 3 months after testifying, 7 months after testifying, and after the disposition of the cases. A matched-pair design (matching children on key demographic and case characteristics) was used to compare 60 children who testified at any proceeding (competency hearing, preliminary hearing, pretrial hearing, or trial) with 60 children who did not testify at any hearing.

- An Office of Juvenile Justice and Delinquency Prevention-funded study in four jurisdictions that replicated the North Carolina study on a much larger sample of children (256) with a focus on children who testified in criminal court. Instruments were administered shortly after the case was referred to the prosecutor and again 7 to 9 months later.

Findings

Differences in findings from the three studies do not allow a conclusive finding as to whether testifying harms or benefits sexually abused children. The Denver study found that testifying may impede the improvement process for some children while the North Carolina study found that testifying may enhance the recovery of some children. The different findings may have been the result of the different proceedings at which children testified. The children in the North Carolina study testified in child protection proceedings while the children in the Denver study testified in criminal court, a much more adversarial system.

Similarities across the three studies include:

- Children scored high on measures of stress and anxiety at the initial testing.

- Children who testified more than once generally did not improve as much as children who never testified or only testified once.

- Most children tended to improve with time whether they testified in court or not.

---

[1] From a Research in Brief, Washington, D.C.: U.S. Department of Justice, National Institute of Justice, April 1994, NCJ 146414.

Implications for Prosecutors, Judges, Law Enforcement, and Victim/Witness Advocates

The Denver study found that children appeared to benefit when the environment of the criminal court was made more child friendly, such as by closing the court to spectators or allowing a parent or other support person to be present when the child testifies. The U.S. Supreme Court has ruled that under special circumstances the criminal process can be modified. This beneficial finding of a child-friendly environment has implications for all the practitioners in the criminal justice system—judges, prosecutors, victim/witness advocates, and law enforcement:

- If children need innovative courtroom procedures to testify, prosecutors should consider making the argument that testifying without these innovations would be too traumatic for the victim.

- Judges should consider whether the children would be sufficiently traumatized to warrant modifying the courtroom.

- Victim/witness advocates should accompany children to court to provide comfort and support, especially when the parent is unable, or unwilling, to do so.

- Children may also benefit when law enforcement interviews children in a child-friendly place (or room) rather than in a frightening police station environment.

Study results also suggest how prosecutors and victim advocates can aid in children's mental health recovery:

- Maternal support was positively associated with children's mental health improvement. The North Carolina study found that mothers who were given help with their own emotional stress were better able to help their children recover. Prosecutors as well as victim/advocates can assist by explaining the criminal process to mothers and by referring those who are stressed to mental health counseling.

- In each of the three studies, children who testified more than once were found to recover more slowly than those who testified only once. Prosecutors should consider limiting the child's testimony to one proceeding, if at all possible.

Selected Findings and Implications Drawn From

Techniques for Improving Children's Testimony

by Debra Whitcomb[2]

Purpose of Research

To identify techniques that can improve children's ability to communicate as witnesses without impairing the validity of the children's stories. The research can be divided into three main areas: Interviewing Techniques, Communication Enhancement Techniques, and Courtroom Preparation Techniques.

Interviewing Techniques

Practitioners increasingly are asked to defend their interviewing techniques regarding allegations of child sexual abuse. These techniques include the use of anatomically detailed dolls and leading questions, which assist in gaining information from children who are reluctant or unable to describe their experience.

---

[2] From *Child Victims as Witnesses: What the Research Says*, Newton, MA: Education Development Center, Inc., 1993.

Anatomically Detailed Dolls. Several studies suggest that the use of dolls helps children communicate what happened to them:

- One study revealed that twice as many children identified suspected perpetrators when using dolls than when not using the dolls. Dolls were very helpful for children under the age of 3, but some children provided no information even after the doll was used (Leventhal et al., 1989).

- Another study suggested that dolls may be more helpful for older children than for younger children in eliciting correct and truthful responses (Goodman and Aman, 1990).

- Critics suggested that the use of dolls places unnatural and increased attention on body parts, so that abused children might display sexually explicit behaviors (Wakefield and Underwager, 1988). Others point out that research does not support that claim and suggest that there is no evidence that the dolls disturb children in any way.

Leading Questions. Another controversial interviewing technique is the use of leading questions. Critics claim that leading questions direct the child's story. Often, however, leading questions are the result of the interviewer making unjustified assumptions prior to posing a question. Studies in this area found:

- Specific questions elicited more information from children than general questions but specific questions also increased the risk of inaccurate information (Dent, 1991).

- Although direct and specific questions increased the risk of false information, there was an even greater risk that not asking direct questions would leave vital information regarding touch unreported (Saywitz et al., 1991).

- Repeated leading questioning influenced children 5 and 6 years old, especially if the questions were ambiguous. Factors identified as affecting responses to leading questions were delay since the event, repeated suggestions by persons of authority, and leading questions being posed by more than one interviewer. In addition, younger children appeared to be much more vulnerable to these types of questions (Goodman and Clarke-Stewart, 1991).

Communication Enhancement Techniques

Interviewers should try to phrase questions in a developmentally sensitive manner. When interviewing a child who may have been sexually abused, interviewers need to be aware that children:

- Think in concrete terms.
- Do not organize their thoughts logically.
- Have limited understanding of space, distance, and time.
- Have a complex understanding of truth and lying.
- See the world egocentrically.
- Have a limited attention span.
- Have varying degrees of comfort with strangers (Waterman, 1986).

It is recommended that interviewers turn to the child's caretaker for better understanding of any idiosyncratic responses the child may provide (Melton and Thompson, 1987). While children's ages may be the same, their positions in the developmental process may differ. Caretakers should be consulted for more individual information about the child.

Courtroom Preparation Techniques

Research reveals that as children get older they gain a better understanding of the legal system. Programs have been developed to assist children in understanding the system, which may include using the following:

- Tours of courtrooms and introductions to key court personnel.
- Coloring or activity books.
- Miniature-sized courtrooms with movable figures and furniture.
- Videotapes explaining the court process.

Implications for Practitioners

When interviewing children who may have been sexually abused, it is recommended that the interviewer:

- Supplement use of anatomically detailed dolls with other interviewing techniques, rather than focusing solely upon the dolls.
- Use both general and direct interview questions but avoid repeated leading questions.
- Consult the child's primary caretaker about the child's language skills and idiosyncratic responses, and make sure the questions are appropriate for the child's developmental stage.
- Be aware of the extent of the child's knowledge of the legal process and take the time necessary to educate him or her on the process.

Practitioners would benefit from regular training to update their interviewing skills and to enhance their ability to detect instances of miscommunication between the child being interviewed and the interviewer.

References

Dent, H.R. "Experimental Studies of Interviewing Child Witnesses." In Doris, J. (ed.), *The Suggestibility of Children's Recollections.* Washington, D.C.: American Psychological Association (1991), 138–146.

Goodman, G.S. and A. Clarke-Stewart. "Suggestibility in Children's Testimony: Implications for Sexual Abuse Investigations." In *The Suggestibility of Children's Recollections,* Doris, J. (ed.). Washington, D.C.: American Psychological Association (1991), 92–105.

Goodman, G.S., and C. Aman. "Children's Use of Anatomically Detailed Dolls to Recount an Event." *Child Development,* 61 (1990), 1859–1871.

Leventhal, J.M., Hamilton, J., Rekedal, S., Tebano-Micci, A., and C. Eyster. "Anatomically Correct Dolls Used in Interviews of Young Children Suspected of Having Been Sexually Abused." *Pediatrics,* 84 (1989), 900–906.

Melton, G.B. and R.A. Thompson. "Detours to Less Traveled Paths in Child Witness Research" In Ceci, S. J., Toglia, M.P., and D.F. Ross (eds.), *Children's Eye-witness Memory.* New York: Springer-Verlag (1987), 217–218.

Saywitz, K., Goodman, G., Nicholas, E., and S. Moan. "Children's Memories of a Physical Examination Involving Genital Touch: Implications for Reports of Child Sexual Abuse." *Journal of Consulting and Clinical Psychology,* 59(5) (1991), 682–691.

Wakefield, H., and R. Underwager. *Accusations of Child Sexual Abuse.* Springfield, IL: Charles C. Thomas (1988), 202–210.

Waterman, J. "Developmental Considerations" In MacFarlane, K., and J. Waterman et al. (eds.), *Sexual Abuse of Young Children.* New York: The Guilford Press (1986), 15–29.

Findings and Implications Drawn From

Effects of Cognitive Interviewing and Practice on Children's Recall Performance

by Karen J. Saywitz, R. Edward Geiselman, and Gail K. Bornstein[3]

Purpose of Research

To refine and evaluate the modified version of the cognitive interview for children originally designed by Geiselman and Padilla; to evaluate the effects of practicing cognitive interview techniques before the interview; and to evaluate the completeness and accuracy of reports from children who participated in the staged event compared with those who only witnessed it.

Methods

In two studies, 132 children were interviewed about staged activities. In one study, the staged event centered on a private encounter between an unfamiliar man (played by the research assistant) and two children. Games involving touching were played (such as Simon Says) and one of the children in each pair wore a costume. Pictures were taken with an "instamatic" camera. One child played the observer and one child the participant.

In the first study, 20 children between the ages of 7 and 8 and another group of 20 between the ages of 10 and 11 were randomly assigned to either the cognitive or standard interview condition and also were randomly assigned to play the participant versus the observer. In the second study, 34 children aged 8 and 9 and 58 aged 11 and 12 were assigned to one of three interview conditions: cognitive interviewing with practice, cognitive interviewing without practice, and rapport building followed by standard police interviewing techniques.

Interviewers who were off-duty detectives from the Los Angeles County Sheriff's Department were randomly assigned to conduct the cognitive interview. They were not provided information about the staged event.

In both studies, children participated in a staged event and were later interviewed. The scenarios were conducted at a local school and videotaped so the children's statements could be compared with what actually took place. The children were interviewed 2 days after the staged event. Both the cognitive and standard police interviews began with rapport building with the child. Interviewers in the standard interview used questioning procedures that they normally use with children that began with an open-ended question asking the children to describe what happened. Those in the cognitive interviewing condition were trained in the use of cognitive memory retrieval techniques.

Findings

The transcribed taped interviews were analyzed in terms of five dependent variables: (1) number of correct facts recalled, (2) number of incorrect items recalled, (3) number of questions asked about the staged event, (4) total time taken to conduct the interview, and (5) number of rapport exchanges preceding questioning. The analysis yielded the following:

- The older children recalled significantly more correct facts than the younger children did.

- For all age groups, the cognitive interview significantly increased the number of correct facts recalled over the standard interview.

---

[3] From *Journal of Applied Psychology*, 77(5) (1992), 744–756.

- Children who were bystanders made more errors than those who were participants. However, they did not differ on number of correct facts recalled.

- The younger children produced significantly more incorrect items than the older children did.

- The average number of questions asked did not differ significantly as a function of age of the child or whether the child was a witness or participant.

- The length of the interview was the same for the older and younger children. Cognitive interviews took about 5 minutes longer to conduct than standard interviews in the first study, but in the second study, there were no significant differences.

- Cognitive interviewing with practice was superior to cognitive interviewing without practice and both were superior to standard police interview techniques. Practice with these novel interviewing techniques prior to the interview produced a significantly greater number of correct pieces of information recalled.

Implications for Criminal Justice Officials

Recollections of school-age children can be improved through cognitive interviewing, which becomes even more effective when:

- Interviewers and children become practiced with cognitive interviewing techniques.

- Interviewers receive training—a critical aspect to the success of cognitive interviewing techniques. Important elements to successful training are role-playing, critique of style, and experienced and proficient cognitive interviewing trainers.

Findings and Implications Drawn From

The Use of Closed-Circuit Television and Videotaped Testimony in Child Sexual Abuse Trials: An Evaluation of BJA's Funding Program

by Sharon G. Elstein, Barbara E. Smith, Howard Davidson, Donald Rebovich, Kathy Free, Mark Ells, and Caren Sempel[4]

Purpose of Research

In 1993, the Bureau of Justice Assistance announced that funding was available to States to provide assistance in purchasing equipment and training in the use of closed-circuit television and/or videotape equipment in child sexual abuse trials. The National Institute of Justice funded the American Bar Association and the American Prosecutors Research Institute to evaluate the impact of the BJA projects.

Methods

The project's methods included: (1) a telephone survey of the 26 States receiving BJA funds; (2) a follow-on indepth telephone survey of jurisdictions to assess the effectiveness of the technologies; (3) a 50-State legal analysis including an analysis of appellate cases; and (4) site studies of four States that have implemented a promising strategy for others to replicate, either in distribution, administration,

---

[4] From an Executive Summary submitted to the National Institute of Justice, May 1996, NIJ grant #94–IJ–CX–0054 to the American Bar Association. Elstein, Smith, and Davidson represented the American Bar Association on this project; Rebovich, Free, Ells, and Sempel represented the American Prosecutors Research Institute.

or installation of equipment, or in providing training on legal, interview, or technical setup skills.

Findings

For the 26 States that received BJA funding, the researchers found the following:

- In compliance with BJA requirements, the States conducted a needs assessment to determine how to distribute the technologies, but many States elected an informal, as opposed to a formal, assessment process.

- Most States elected to distribute the funds on a countywide, as opposed to a statewide, basis.

- Funds were fairly equally divided between the purchase of closed-circuit and videotape equipment. Many States also expended BJA dollars on training.

- Many States experienced delays in using BJA funds and had to overcome funding implementation obstacles.

- High marks were given to the impact and usefulness of both videotape and closed-circuit equipment. Most prosecutors said that the technologies were available and useful when needed. Prosecutors generally perceived that the technologies reduced trauma to the child. It was emphasized that closed-circuit television or the introduction of videotape interviews is needed only in a minority of cases and that "live" testimony of children is preferred. But on those rare occasions when a child simply cannot testify except on camera, these technologies were considered an invaluable tool.

- Despite obstacles to the implementation of BJA funding, the States persevered and implemented the use of closed-circuit television and videotape equipment and/or provided training. Many States were creative in the use of the funds and stretched the limited BJA dollars (approximately $38,000 to each of the 26 States) by combining these dollars with other Federal or State funds targeted for children's issues. Consequently, they were able to accomplish much more than would have been possible with a single funding source.

Implications for Federal Funding Agencies

Federal agencies should consider the benefit of requiring matching funds from States to demonstrate their interest in pursuing programs supported by Federal dollars. BJA required jurisdictions to demonstrate State support for the projects by making a hard match of 25 percent a condition of the award. Limited Federal funds can be used very effectively in supporting States with a demonstrated history of ongoing programs focused on a particular strategy for prosecuting child sexual abuse cases. States with a history of supporting closed-circuit television and videotape technologies were able to combine the BJA funding with other Federal and State funds and create an ambitious program.

Implications for Criminal Justice Planners and Professionals

The researchers offered the following suggestions with respect to training, multiagency cooperation, resources, and equipment:

- Localities should take advantage of the strengths of various agencies within their jurisdiction when implementing child abuse programs. In particular, they should look to existing child advocacy centers and multidisciplinary teams, which investigate and prosecute child sexual abuse allegations, to help implement such programs. The existing open communication across agencies involved in multidisciplinary teams may help ensure the success of such efforts.

The input of prosecutors, judges, law enforcement, investigators, defense attorneys, victim/witness advocates, doctors, mental health workers, and other professionals involved with abused children can help considerably in implementing closed-circuit television and videotape projects.

- Training provided to a broad spectrum of criminal justice professionals should be a critical component of any effort to implement new strategies—or to expand existing strategies—for prosecuting child abuse cases. With respect to the closed-circuit and videotape projects, training is important on technical aspects of the equipment, but more important on the legal requirements for using the technologies and forensic interviewing skills with abused children.

- To maximize resources, States should consider employing mobile units if special technologies will be used in a minority of cases. Statewide or regionwide mobile units can be effective in ensuring that closed-circuit television equipment is available to any court where it is needed, while at the same time eliminating the waste involved in having the equipment lie dormant. States may implement a program where small counties can access videotape equipment at facilities designed for taping testimony/interviews, such as at local child advocacy centers.

- Closed-circuit television and videotape technologies are firmly established in the criminal justice system as appropriate for use in special cases. The researchers recommended that States:

    — Continue to plan for the use of closed-circuit television and videotape equipment.

    — Ensure that these technologies are available for appropriate cases in counties across the State.

    — Ensure that those using the technologies are adequately trained in technical and substantive issues related to their use.

Selected Findings and Implications Drawn From

Children's Testimony and Their Perceptions of Stress in and out of the Courtroom

by Karen J. Saywitz and Rebecca Nathanson[5]

Purpose of Research

To explore the effect of the courtroom environment on the quality of evidence given by children and the level of system-induced stress on children.

Methods

Children were assigned to two conditions, one in which an interview was conducted in the child's school and one in which the interview was conducted in a courtroom. A matched sample was used in which 34 children between the ages of 8 and 10 were assigned to each of the groups based on socioeconomic status and age.

The activity the children were to remember was a 30-minute staged event during which an adult male taught the children about the parts and functions of the human body. A structured interview was used to evaluate free and probed recall of the staged event 2 weeks after the staged event. The interview either took place at the school or in a courtroom with actors playing the roles of judge, defense attorney, prosecutor, bailiff, jurors, and spectators.

---

[5] From *Child Abuse and Neglect*, 17(5) (1993), 613–622.

Findings

Comparisons between children who were questioned about the staged event in the courtroom versus at school found:

- Children interviewed at school recalled significantly more correct items than children interviewed at court on the free recall part of the questioning.

- For probed questions, children interviewed at court gave significantly more incorrect responses to probed questions than children interviewed at school.

- Children interviewed at school made significantly fewer errors on misleading questions than did children interviewed at court.

- Children interviewed at court perceived their experience as significantly more stressful on some of the measures than children interviewed at school.

- The more stressful children perceived their court experience to be, the fewer correct items they reported in free recall.

Implications for Judges, Law Enforcement Officers, Victim/Witness Advocates, and Prosecutors*

The following implications present suggestions to help reduce children's stress and anxiety associated with interviews and the court setting:

- Interviewing children in places where they feel comfortable may yield fuller, more accurate accounts than interviewing them in a potentially frightening place, such as a police station, prosecutor's office, or formal victim/witness office.

- Victim/witness advocates and prosecutors can help reduce stress on children who must testify in court by walking them through the court process in a courtroom. This would also help reduce children's fear of the setting. Allowing a child to hold a familiar toy may also minimize the strangeness of the court setting.

- To reduce children's anxiety about the court setting, it might be helpful for a judge to meet the child in the courtroom before the hearing to explain the proceeding in less frightening terms. If there would be a conflict for the trial judge to do this, another judge might substitute, or the explanation might be given right before the hearing begins with the lawyers present.

---

* These implications are not explicit in the presentation but appear to follow from the findings.

Prosecution of Child Abuse and Neglect Cases

Selected Findings and Implications Drawn From

The Prosecution of Child Sexual and Physical Abuse Cases

by Barbara E. Smith and Sharon Goretsky Elstein[6]

Purpose of Research

To determine how cases of child physical and sexual abuse are being prosecuted and to examine the outcomes of child sexual abuse cases in criminal courts across the country.

Methods

Project staff employed two methods of data collection: a telephone survey of 600 prosecutors nationwide regarding child physical and sexual abuse (conducted in 1990 and 1991) and the collection of information from nearly 1,000 case files of sexual abuse in 10 counties (for cases disposed of between 1988 and 1992; dates of disposition varied from county to county).

Findings

The study compared the findings from the national telephone survey of prosecutors with the nearly 1,000 case files of child sexual abuse. Based on the telephone interviews and the case file review, the researchers found:

- Prosecutors noted an increase in fondling offenses in the 2 years prior to the survey. The case data revealed that 22 percent of the cases involved *only* fondling offenses.

- Prosecutors reported seeing more cases involving younger children in the 2 years prior to the survey. The case file data confirmed that many cases with young children are being prosecuted. The researchers found more than one-tenth (14 percent) of the victims were age 5 or younger.

- Many prosecutors noted an increase in the number or proportion of perpetrators using alcohol or drugs in the 2 years prior to the survey. In the case data, the researchers found that 18 percent of the defendants used alcohol and 6 percent used drugs during (or shortly prior to) the sexual assault.

- Prosecutors stated that they see very few cases of child sexual abuse by strangers, and noted a rise in the number of cases with step-parents, romantic partners of the parent, and biological parents in the 2 years prior to the survey. The case data document the prevalence of abuse by perpetrators known to the child. In only 6 percent of the cases were victims abused by strangers while 32 percent were abused by a parent or parental figure.

- The majority of prosecutors stated during the telephone survey that they do not divert child sexual abuse offenders at any stage in the process. Of the cases that passed indictment, only 3 percent of the offenders were diverted prior to conviction, according to the case data.

- Prosecutors stated during the telephone survey that the most likely sentence in child sexual abuse cases was more than 1 year of incarceration, with the next most likely

---

[6] From a Final Report, American Bar Association's Center on Children and the Law, submitted to the National Center on Child Abuse and Neglect, September 30, 1993.

sentence being probation. In the case data, the researchers found that 59 percent of offenders were given a jail or prison sentence and 64 percent were given probation (these were not mutually exclusive; 14 percent of the offenders who received incarcerated time were sentenced to a period of probation following their incarceration).

Implications for Law Enforcement, Prosecutors, Child Protective Services, and the Medical Community

Prosecutors seldom see child physical abuse cases compared with the frequency with which they see sexual abuse cases. (Indeed, that was why the researchers examined only child sexual abuse cases in the case study; not enough counties could be located that prosecuted sufficient numbers of physical abuse cases to be included in the study.) The researchers concluded that prosecutors should have the opportunity to review many more child physical abuse cases to assess the feasibility of criminal prosecution. Strategies such as public education; training of law enforcement, child protective services, and medical authorities to identify cases appropriate for prosecutorial review; and training of prosecutors to prosecute these cases, hold promise for increasing the frequency with which prosecutors accept child physical abuse cases for prosecution.

Implications for Law Enforcement and Prosecutors

The study found that the use of "special techniques" such as closed-circuit television, videotaped testimony, and anatomically correct dolls is not needed in most child sexual abuse investigations and prosecutions. In most cases, careful preparation of the witness will be sufficient, but these special tools are very important in the limited number of cases where children cannot talk about the abuse without using them.

Implications for the Criminal Justice and the Substance Abuse Therapeutic Communities

Defendants in the cases studied frequently were using alcohol or drugs during the abusive incident or had a history of alcohol or drug abuse. In light of the large number of child molesters who have alcohol or drug abuse problems, criminal justice officials (judges, prosecutors, probation officers, and defense attorneys) and the substance abuse therapeutic communities need to consider implementing a comprehensive treatment approach for convicted child molesters.

Implications for Public Education

In the cases studied, the child almost always knew the defendant (often a parent or parental figure). Public attention should continue to focus on the dangers of children being molested by strangers, but just as important, the general public should be educated to the reality that more than 90 percent of all child sexual abuse offenders are individuals known to the children they abuse. This is especially important in criminal justice cases. Members of the public make up jury pools and increased public awareness that child sexual abuse is often perpetrated by individuals close to the child would help in prosecuting these cases.

Selected Findings and Implications Drawn From

Prosecuting Child Physical Abuse Cases: A Case Study in San Diego

by Barbara E. Smith[7]

Purpose of Research

To learn via a case study in San Diego, California, about a coordinated response to the prosecution of child physical abuse cases and to help other communities replicate the model.

Methods

The case study included extensive interviews with child protective services, law enforcement, prosecutors, and staff at Children's Hospital as well as data collected from 15 case files.

Findings

San Diego has a multiagency approach to prosecuting child physical abuse cases with several distinctive characteristics:

- The police department and the district attorney's office each have specialized units with specially trained staff members. Child Protective Services provides a 6- to 8-week training program on investigating child abuse and neglect cases for newly hired workers.

- The roles and responsibilities of each agency are delineated in a memorandum of agreement to ensure that one agency does not interfere with the work of another.

- The medical community plays a pivotal role in collecting and interpreting evidence of child physical abuse.

- Multiagency meetings among prosecutors, law enforcement, child protective services, and the medical community foster coordination of individual cases and provide a forum for discussing general issues.

Implications for Prosecutors, Law Enforcement, Child Protective Workers, and the Medical Communities

Based on the case files, interviews, and other study data, the researchers drew the following practical implications:

- Any case in which a child's injury appears suspicious should be carefully scrutinized to determine if criminal action is warranted. The common assumption that prosecutors will reject physical injury cases because they are too difficult to prove needs to be changed.

What can be done to facilitate prosecutors receiving and reviewing more physical abuse cases? Public education, training of criminal justice and medical authorities, and a willingness to take on the challenge of cases that are difficult to prove are strategies that hold promise for increasing the frequency with which prosecutors accept physical child abuse cases for prosecution.

- A coordinated multiagency response among child protective services, the police, the medical community, and the prosecutor is recommended.

The successful prosecution of criminal cases depends on the effectiveness of the prosecutor *and* on the quality of the investigation conducted before the prosecutor receives the case. Indeed, the early investigative work can make or break the case for the prosecutor. Therefore, it is important that the medical, child protective service, and law enforcement communities look for signs that a child's injuries were intentional and conduct sound investigations that

---

[7] From a Research in Brief, Washington, D.C.: U.S. Department of Justice, National Institute of Justice and the Office of Juvenile Justice and Delinquency Prevention, June 1995, NCJ 152978.

will preserve the important evidence for the prosecution and defense.

- Specialization, coupled with extensive training, should be given strong consideration as an important foundation for building sound prosecution cases.

In San Diego, specialization within the police department and the prosecutor's office was important in several respects. First, specialization created a core of professionals who received the best available training on child abuse investigations and prosecutions. This is especially important in physical abuse cases where the key evidence often rests on complicated medical evidence. It also facilitates the acquisition of knowledge on the psychology of child abusers and the dynamics in intrafamilial abuse, so common in these cases. Second, specialization allows law enforcement and prosecutors to build an extensive level of experience in investigating and prosecuting child abuse cases. Third, specialization results in a small number of law enforcement officers and prosecutors handing child abuse cases. Because the number of personnel is small, professionals have the opportunity to form close-knit interpersonal working relationships.

- Public education designed to reach future potential jurors about the nature of child physical abuse should be given priority.

The San Diego study leaves little doubt that child physical abuse cases will remain difficult to prosecute unless jurors are enlightened about the dynamics involved in these types of cases. Ten years ago, juror disbelief that child sexual abuse occurred was common, but that has begun to change with public education (although the fallout from some highly publicized cases appears to have created some degree of backlash among the public). Public education in the area of physical abuse needs to reach the level that public education has on sexual abuse. Unless that happens, it is likely that prosecutors will continue to confront jurors who are reluctant to convict.

Selected Findings and Implications Drawn From

Justice System Processing of Child Abuse and Neglect Cases

edited by Noy S. Davis and Susan J. Wells[8]

Purpose of Research

To better understand the civil and criminal justice system processing of child abuse and neglect cases; to determine the types of coordination activities that result in more effective justice system processing; and to determine the potential for tracking cases through the child protective services and legal systems to facilitate case coordination and allow for the study of case processing and court outcomes.

Methods

The research had four unique components: (1) a national telephone survey of child protective services, law enforcement, and court personnel in 41 counties; (2) a case study comparison of the processing of child maltreatment cases in two sites; (3) a case study of one site that aggressively prosecutes cases of child physical abuse; and (4) a prospective case tracking study in one site in which 450 cases were prospectively

---

[8] From an Executive Summary submitted to the National Institute of Justice and the Office of Juvenile Justice and Delinquency Prevention, under NIJ grant #92–IJ–CX–K041, in cooperation with the National Center on Child Abuse and Neglect, by the American Bar Association Center on Children and the Law; Westat, Inc.; James Bell Associates; and the Research Triangle Institute, February 1996.

tracked from the time of the report through the juvenile and criminal justice systems. The project took place between 1993 and 1995.

Findings

Findings from the national telephone survey revealed that:

- Slightly less than one-half of the law enforcement agencies surveyed for the study had specialized units to investigate reports of child abuse and neglect.

- There were substantial differences among the 41 counties in the extent of communication between law enforcement and child protective service agencies. The most frequent pattern called for law enforcement to cross-report to child protective services. Less than half of the counties reported using a multidisciplinary approach.

- Respondents noted no established criteria guiding the prosecutor's decision to drop, plea bargain, or try a case. More than two-thirds of the counties had a specialized prosecution unit to handle child abuse and neglect cases.

- Communication between the prosecutor's office and child protective services was rated as minimal in most counties.

- Several technical factors were identified as inhibitors to the tracking of cases from one agency to another such as inconsistent information maintained in databases; differing geographical boundaries and jurisdictions; widely varying timeframes for case actions; and the lack of a system for giving feedback on case outcomes to other agencies.

Findings from the case study comparison of the processing of child maltreatment cases in two sites showed that:

- In cases that involved both juvenile and criminal proceedings, there were conflicting opinions as to whether the timing of the dual proceedings had any negative impact on the outcome of either proceeding.

- In both sites there was neither routine, direct communication between the juvenile and criminal court judges handling the case nor any automatic exchange of records or information between the two systems.

- Cases involving child abuse and neglect were handled in an idiosyncratic fashion.

Findings from the case study of a county that aggressively prosecutes cases of child physical abuse are presented in the summary of a National Institute of Justice Research in Brief, *The Prosecution of Child Physical Abuse Cases: A Case Study in San Diego*, which appears elsewhere in this document.

Findings from the prospective study of the tracking of child maltreatment cases in one jurisdiction showed that:

- Sexual abuse cases had the highest predicted level of criminal prosecution.

- Cases involving female victims were more likely to be criminally prosecuted than those involving male victims.

- Cases involving victims ages 7 to 12 were much more likely to be prosecuted than cases involving older or younger children.

- Physical neglect cases were the most likely to result in dependency court filings.

- Multiple relationships, that is, offenders who had abused their own children as well as another child, were most likely to result in prosecution.

Implications for Improving Case Processing

The researchers offered the following recommendations:

- The development of training system models suitable to different environments may be the most effective approach to developing management information and tracking systems in this field.

- Standard definitions for data elements would be useful.

- Implementation of practices and procedures to guide communication strategies across agencies is needed.

- The formation of common goals would be an important step in establishing interagency communication and trust.

- It is important to coordinate not only juvenile and criminal court processing, but also other proceedings that may be related to these cases, such as child support, domestic violence, custody, or divorce proceedings.

- Professionalizing law enforcement, child protective services agencies, and prosecution, combined with manageable caseloads, may help improve the coordination among the staff of these agencies. In addition, the negative impact of frequent staff turnover needs to be addressed as a deterrent to fostering coordination.

Findings and Implications Drawn From

Coordinating Criminal and Juvenile Court Proceedings in Child Maltreatment Cases

by Debra Whitcomb and Mark Hardin[9]

Purpose of Research

To conduct a national assessment of the coordination of criminal and juvenile court proceedings in child maltreatment cases. Intrafamilial child maltreatment cases often involve simultaneous criminal and juvenile court proceedings. The juvenile court handles the child protection proceeding, which is designed to protect the child, assist the family, and provide the child with a permanent home. The purpose of the criminal proceeding is to protect the public, deter future crime, punish, and rehabilitate. Not only are the goals of each proceeding different, but they can be incompatible, inefficient, and detrimental to the child and family. For example, when juvenile court actions precede the criminal matter, as is customarily the case, the alleged offenders are at risk. Information they provide to comply with juvenile court treatment plans, such as their involvement with therapy, can be used against them in subsequent prosecutions.

Methods

Two research components were employed in this study: (1) a nationally representative telephone survey of prosecutors and child protection attorneys and (2) site visits to four jurisdictions. For the phone survey, 150 counties were sampled with two primary respondents in each county: a prosecutor with responsibility for criminal child maltreatment cases and an attorney representing the child protection agency. Overall, 103 prosecutors and 59 child protection attorneys responded to the phone survey. Four counties were chosen for indepth court coordination study: Chittenden County (Burlington), Vermont; Tompkins County (Ithaca), New York; Santa Clara County (San Jose), California; and Hawaii County (Hilo and Kona), Hawaii.

---

[9] From an Executive Summary under National Institute of Justice grant # 92–IJ–CX–K034 to the Education Development Center, Inc., and the American Bar Association Center on Children and the Law. The Full Report published in 1995 is available through the National Criminal Justice Reference Service, NCJ 161835.

Findings

Research from the phone survey revealed:

- A high proportion of respondents were satisfied with the degree of coordination between the two systems and their efforts to achieve this level of coordination.

- Responding prosecutors estimated that 60 percent of their child maltreatment cases were concurrently involved in juvenile court proceedings. Sexual abuse was the offense category most likely to be involved in both courts.

- Approximately half the attorneys surveyed indicated that dual court cases proceed independently, with no consideration given to case status in the other court.

- There was little concern, particularly among prosecutors, about the need to coordinate between the criminal court and the juvenile court. Some respondents felt that efforts to coordinate would even be inappropriate or counterproductive.

- Survey respondents reported that coordination of cases, which resulted in increased knowledge of cases, had an impact on litigation strategies such as deciding whether or not to pursue a case or negotiate pleas.

- Prosecutors from larger counties were less satisfied with coordination than prosecutors from smaller communities.

Visits to the four sites found:

- The exchange of information between juvenile courts and criminal courts was hampered by confidentiality rules.

- Inconsistent court orders occur infrequently in all four jurisdictions because defense attorneys represent the alleged offender in both courts; probation officers incorporate juvenile court orders into their presentence investigation reports to the criminal court; and criminal court judges mention juvenile court orders in their own orders involving pretrial release or probation.

- Juvenile court proceedings usually proceeded faster than related criminal cases. Respondents were dissatisfied with the conflicting goals of the two courts (rehabilitation/reunification vs. punishment/retribution). Defense counsels were dissatisfied with the statutory protections available to their clients. They regarded "testimonial immunity" statutes (which allow alleged perpetrators to speak freely without fearing that their statements will be used against them in criminal court) as inadequate protection and often advised clients not to testify in juvenile court or participate in therapy.

Based on the study findings, the researchers concluded:

- Although coordination is not consistent across jurisdictions, many agencies work well together during the investigative process.

- It is very important that there be coordination in the litigation between the criminal and juvenile court. With increased coordination between the two types of proceedings comes a decrease in inconsistent and conflicting orders.

- Counsel for the child protection agency and the criminal prosecutor must communicate in order to have successful coordination in child maltreatment proceedings.

Implications for Criminal Justice and Child Protection Authorities

Certain child maltreatment-related cases should be coordinated in the criminal and juvenile courts for several reasons:

- To ensure that both courts have access to complete information.
- To decrease the likelihood of conflicting or inconsistent court orders.
- To avoid unnecessary trauma to child victims.
- To address the conflict that arises when alleged offenders are denied treatment under juvenile court plans for fear that admissions will be used against them in criminal court.

Criminal justice and child protection authorities can increase their coordination by:

- Creating a detailed procedure for working together.
- Establishing good working relationships between counsels.
- Creating multidisciplinary councils and teams.
- Mandating interagency coordination, cooperation, and collaboration.
- Increasing judicial awareness of parallel proceedings in child abuse and neglect cases.

Sentencing

Selected Findings and Implications Drawn From

The Probation Response to Child Sexual Abuse Offenders: How Is it Working?

by Barbara E. Smith, Susan W. Hillenbrand, and Sharon R. Goretsky[10]

Purpose of Research

To explore what court-ordered probation in child sexual abuse cases means in terms of prosecution, sentencing, supervision, treatment, and revocation or success rates. Previous studies had shown that probation is a common or perhaps even the primary sentence for persons convicted of child sexual abuse.

Methods

The study employed two methods: (1) a national telephone survey of chief probation officers in 100 randomly selected counties, supplemented by a mail survey of State directors of probation or other relevant State representatives, and (2) site visits to Travis County, Texas; Salt Lake County, Utah; St. Joseph County, Indiana; and the State of Maine for discussions with more than 60 judges, probation officers, prosecutors, defense attorneys, therapists, and victim advocates.

Findings

Telephone and mail survey results revealed:

- Fewer than half of the county probation departments had special regulations or guidelines for dealing with probationers convicted of child sexual abuse.

- Probation caseloads were too high to supervise child sexual abuse probationers adequately.

- Staff training on child sexual abuse was often inadequate, and relatively few probation departments had specialized units to deal with these cases.

- The average probation sentence in a majority of the jurisdictions was 3 to 5 years, a period thought "about right" by the chief probation officers.

- Most probation officers were satisfied with the specificity judges used in ordering special conditions.

- Psychological counseling was the special condition most often ordered. "Stay away" orders were also common.

- Public mental health programs commonly provided psychological treatment, although private counselors were also frequently used.

- Few jurisdictions had sufficient numbers of good treatment programs, either for those who were indigent or for those with the means to pay. Few departments had standards for treatment programs.

- Most child sexual abuse probationers were required to report to their probation officers in person; surprise and collateral contacts were also common.

- Few child sexual abusers were brought back to court for reoffending or other "major" violations.

---

[10] From a Final Report to the State Justice Institute under grant #SJI–88–11J–E–015 to the American Bar Association, January 1990.

Practitioner interview results revealed:

- There was no consensus about whether individuals who sexually abuse children within the nuclear (or extended) family should be treated differently than other child sexual abusers.
- Most child sexual abuse cases were handled by negotiated plea rather than by trial.
- Judges usually followed the sentencing recommendations in the presentence report.
- Offenders thought to be amenable to treatment (i.e., those who admitted to at least some sort of abuse) were likely to be sentenced to probation, sometimes accompanied by short periods of shock incarceration in a local jail. Those who denied the abuse were likely to receive prison sentences.
- There was no consensus as to the optimal length of probation (the shortest was 2 years, the longest 10). Practitioners in jurisdictions with shorter probation sentences tended to think that all that could be done for the offender could be accomplished in several years. Those in jurisdictions with longer probation sentences tended to think that lengthier supervision would at least reduce reoffending for a longer time, and might even extend the length of time between the end of probation and reoffense. Regardless of the length of probation, however, there was little confidence that abuse would not reoccur after probation terminated and probationers were no longer closely watched.
- By far, the most common offense-specific condition of probation was treatment for the offender's sexual orientation to children. Orders to stay away from the victim or other minor children were also common.
- Residential halfway houses were used in two of the sites; intensive or maximum supervision was used in all, at least initially. Such supervision included collateral contacts with the probationer's employer, therapist, family members, and associates; unannounced visits to the probationer's home or place of employment; and frequent in-person meetings between the probation officer and the probationer.
- Specialized probation officers with reduced caseloads and some training on issues relating to child sexual abuse supervised child sexual abuse probationers in three of the sites.
- Child sexual abuse probationers were generally required to sign waivers of confidentiality allowing their probation officers to receive progress reports from treatment providers and to obtain otherwise confidential information from employers and government agencies.
- Lack of treatment alternatives and long waiting lists were common. Almost universally, practitioners cited the need for more therapists and more alternative therapy settings—in halfway houses, prisons, and jails.
- Coordination between the treatment provider and probation officer was considered critical to the successful treatment of the offender; unfortunately, such coordination was often precluded by probation officers' heavy caseloads.

Based on their study findings, the researchers concluded:

- Child sexual abuse probationers require special supervision by probation officers.
- Close coordination between probation officers and treatment providers is important.
- A variety of sentencing options and approaches are necessary to address the needs of all child sexual abuse offenders.
- "Successful" and "unsuccessful" termination of probation and treatment needs to be better defined and documented.

Implications for all Criminal Justice Officials

Prosecutors, defense attorneys, judges, and probation officers should inform themselves or be trained about available treatment options, eligibility requirements, treatment regimens, and waiting lists of various programs, both in the community and in correctional facilities.

Implications for Judges

Judges faced with the uncomfortable sentencing choice of treatment without incarceration or incarceration without treatment might consider short-term shock incarceration, followed by probation with treatment. (Shock incarceration was a system whereby judges would sentence offenders to a lengthy prison term and then bring them back to court after several months were served. At that point, offenders would be asked if they have had sufficient time to contemplate the severity of their crime and its affect on their victims. If they responded affirmatively, they would be offered the chance to be placed on probation in lieu of returning to prison.)

Implications for Probation Officials

Probation departments could establish specialized units to monitor child sexual abuse offenders. These units would:

- Reduce caseloads to allow more careful monitoring.
- Establish guidelines for frequent contact between the probationer and the probation officer, including surprise visits and collateral contacts with the probationer's therapist, employer, family members, and associates.
- Provide intensive training on issues related to child sexual abuse and the monitoring of abusers.

Probation departments and officers could:

- Require probationers to sign confidentiality waivers to facilitate access to relevant information and allow meaningful communication between treatment providers and probation officers.
- Receive joint training with treatment providers to clarify roles and responsibilities and to establish mutually advantageous interactions.
- Communicate with probationers' therapists frequently, by telephone, written communication, and in-person meetings.
- Maintain and distribute to judges and treatment providers statistics on the number of child sexual abuse probationers who successfully and unsuccessfully terminate their periods of probation, including reasons for unsuccessful terminations.

Findings and Implications Drawn From

Managing Adult Sex Offenders in the Community—A Containment Approach

by Kim English, Suzanne Pullen, and Linda Jones[11]

Purpose of Research

To identify how probation and parole agencies manage adult sex offenders and develop a model process for managing adult sex offenders in the community.

Methods

The study had two primary components: a telephone survey and field research. The telephone survey was administered to probation and parole supervisors in 49 States and the District of Columbia. The field research included more than 100 interviews in 13 jurisdictions in Arizona, Colorado, Louisiana, Ohio, Oregon, and Texas. Interviews were conducted with probation and parole officers, defense and prosecuting attorneys, law enforcement personnel, social services workers, sex offender treatment providers, sexual assault victim treatment providers, polygraph examiners, judges, correctional administrators, parole authorities, victim advocates, and sex offenders. In addition to the phone survey and field interviews, a literature review on victim trauma and sex offender management and treatment, a legal analysis of sex offender statutes in 50 States, and a review of documents such as manuals, protocols, and policies were conducted. This research examined the probation and parole response to adult sex offenders whose victims are children as well as adults. Many of these findings and recommendations apply particularly to adults who sexually abuse children.

Findings

Telephone survey results indicated:

- In 1994, about one-third of the probation and parole agencies had specialized caseloads for managing sex offenders.

- Agencies with specialized caseloads were more likely than other agencies to report a philosophy focusing on victim safety and the use of community safety-related approaches such as special supervision conditions and after-hours monitoring of offenders.

Research into the model process found:

- Public safety, victim protection, and reparation for victims are important components of the model process for managing and containing sex offenders on probation or parole.

- There are three elements of supervision that make up the model community containment process:

    — Treatment to assist the offender in developing internal controls over deviant thoughts.

    — Supervision of the offender by probation and parole officers to exert external controls.

    — Polygraph examinations to obtain complete sexual history information and monitor the offender's behavior for treatment and supervision compliance.

---

[11] From a Research in Brief, Washington, D.C.: U.S. Department of Justice, National Institute of Justice, January 1997, NCJ 163387.

- The model process employs a multidisciplinary approach to dealing with sex offender management.
- The model process recommends clear and consistent public policies.
- The model process includes quality control to monitor current policies and practices and to evaluate the impact of the policies and practices.

Implications

Researchers drew several implications from their findings:

- Professionals who work with sex offenders may experience secondary trauma, that is, emotional or psychological effects on professionals who work with difficult populations such as sex offenders. To deal with secondary trauma, organizations and agencies should provide a safe environment staffed by personnel who understand secondary trauma and the dynamics of sex offenders. Professionals who work with sex offenders would need to receive direct training as well as cross-training among different agencies on a regular basis.
- The model process should be tailored to the needs of each community. However, the most important factor—public and victim safety—must always be a high priority.
- Supervision plans should be individualized for each offender and the offender's particular risks.
- Individualized supervision plans should restrict or bar certain activities that provide access to victims.
- Short-term sanctions should be developed for sex offenders who engage in high-risk behavior. These could include short-term mental health and jail holds, extra counseling, halfway house confinement, and fines.
- Agencies and organizations that deal with sex offenses should communicate and collaborate with each other.
- Sex offenders who are under supervision should be required to participate in approved treatment programs.
- For some sex offenders, long-term or lifetime supervision sentences should be considered.

Impact of Domestic Violence on Children's Behavior

Selected Findings and Implications Drawn From

Children of Battered Women: The Relation of Child Behavior to Family Violence and Maternal Stress

by David A. Wolfe, Peter Jaffe, Susan Kaye Wilson, and Lydia Zak[12]

Purpose of Research

To measure the impact of domestic violence on children in terms of behavior problems and social competence.

Methods

The study included 142 mothers and 198 children ranging from 4 to 16 years of age. Comparisons were made between 102 children in violent families drawn from shelters and 96 children from nonviolent families drawn from the community. For the mothers, the assessment measures were the amount of physical violence between partners; the degree of maternal stress and adjustment as measured by the mother's symptoms of emotional and physical health problems; negative life events; and three sociodemographic factors—changes in residences, number of marital separations in the past 2 years, and use of community services to assess the level of family crises. For the children, the assessment measure was a checklist with a parental rating of 20 social competence items and 118 behavior problems.

Findings

The study showed that:

- Significantly more children from violent families scored higher on behavior and competency problems than did children from nonviolent families. In fact, children from violent families had a rate of behavior and social competency problems 2.5 times higher than those from nonviolent families. More than one-quarter of the children from violent families had problems severe enough to fall into the clinical range.

- The association between behavior and social competency problems between those in violent versus nonviolent families was especially strong for boys.

- Children in violent families who were exposed to a higher frequency and intensity of physical violence and whose mothers reported more negative life events, scored higher on behavior and social competency problems than children with lower frequency and intensity of physical violence and whose mothers reported fewer negative life events.

---

[12] From *Journal of Consulting and Clinical Psychology*, 53(5) (1985), 657–665.

Implications for Prosecutors

Domestic violence victims should be asked whether their children are experiencing behavior and competency problems. For those who are, prosecutors should refer the mother to victim assistance, crisis providers, and other support services so that the children's needs are not overlooked.

Implications for Victim Assistance

When providing services to domestic violence victims, inquiries should be made on how the children are coping. Efforts to assist mothers will have a positive bearing on children. Appropriate referrals to short- and long-term services should be made.

Other

Selected Findings and Implications Drawn From

Parental Drug Testing in Child Abuse and Neglect Cases: The Washington, D.C., Experience

by Lisa C. Newmark[13]

Purpose of Research

To provide insight on when parental drug testing was conducted in child abuse and neglect cases and to examine client and court outcomes associated with its use.

Methods

The Family Division of the District of Columbia Superior Court has civil jurisdiction over children named in child maltreatment petitions. The D.C. Family Court judges began referring abuse and neglect cases for drug testing in 1987 to assist courts and social services in identifying and addressing treatment needs. The court's goal is to promote child safety as well as family preservation.

The research compared a matched sample of 169 drug-involved cases that entered the drug testing program from October 1, 1989, to December 31, 1990, with a similar group of 159 drug-involved cases from the same period that did not enter the drug testing program.

Findings

The study identified case services and dispositions that may be associated with the testing program. The author cautions that conclusions are preliminary in light of research methodology limitations. The study found that cases in which the parent(s) participated in drug testing (compared to those that did not), were more likely to experience the following outcomes:

- More frequent court hearings over a shorter time and a shorter overall case processing time.

- Children placed more often with the primary caregiver or other family member than in foster homes or institutions.

- More service referrals to caregivers for drug treatment, child-oriented services, and housing and other basic needs.

- Greater monitoring of visitation, as indicated by the court's practice to grant, revoke, or deny visitation rights.

- Increased parental cooperation with referrals for diagnostic services.

---

[13] From a Final Report to the National Institute of Justice under grant #93–IJ–CX–0042, published by the Urban Institute, December 1995.

Implications for the Criminal Justice System

Drug testing seems to be a promising tool for courts and social services to use in working with child maltreatment cases in which parents are substance abusers. Testing was associated with achieving a number of the courts' and social services agencies' goals, including identifying treatment needs and making service referrals, using family placements and a monitored parental visitation program, and reunifying families.

Other jurisdictions interested in implementing a testing program can benefit from the District of Columbia's experience. When developing such a program, it is critical to enroll the support of all relevant agencies and establish a coordinated approach with strong channels of communication. Policies should be developed, monitored, and revised as needed on specific operational issues, such as testing logistics, case selection and referral mechanisms, testing schedules, program registration, recordkeeping and reporting, and monitoring and sanctioning noncompliance and "dirty" test results.

Jurisdictions interested in implementing drug-testing programs also need to plan for the court and social service resources required by such programs. These include:

- *Court resources.* Testing appears to be associated with more frequent court hearings and shorter case processing times. Courts may need to allocate resources for a more intense approach to case processing.

- *Case management services.* Children of tested parents were placed more frequently with their parents and less frequently in foster homes than were children of nontested parents. As a result, more extensive services may be required for reunited families in order to monitor progress, protect child safety, and promote healthier family functioning in the long term.

- *Service referrals.* Increased referrals to several types of services, not just drug treatment services, were associated with testing. Jurisdictions should allocate sufficient resources to meet the needs of referred cases and courts should coordinate anticipated demands with treatment professionals in the community. This is especially important given that judges and case managers said that inadequate levels of services for drug abuse and other family problems is the biggest obstacle to the restoration of functional families.

- *Case disposition.* There was some evidence that testing is associated with family reunification rather than adoption or termination of parental rights. Should this occur in other jurisdictions implementing drug testing programs, a plan for extensive aftercare services should be implemented to reduce the incidence of repeat maltreatment and the recycling of these cases through the system.

Chapter Two: Research on Legal Interventions in Elder Abuse Cases

While elder abuse has not been examined as extensively as spousal violence and child abuse, research over the past decade has shed some light on elder abuse and resulted in recommendations for improving the response to this problem. However, there is a critical need for more research in this area. This chapter examines studies on the coordination and collaboration between social service and criminal justice systems, as well as research-based recommendations for State courts when dealing with elder abuse.

Coordination and Collaboration

Collaborative and coordinated responses by the various relevant public and private agencies have become increasingly popular strategies when addressing complicated social problems. The two studies presented in this chapter examine working relationships between the social services system and the criminal justice system. The first examines the extent to which formal and informal protocols and joint training exist among State adult protective agencies and law enforcement agencies in 45 States. The second study examines interagency protocols in an effort to improve communication between agencies, increase referrals, and facilitate service plans for victims. In both studies, communication, coordination, and collaboration between social service agencies and the criminal justice system are viewed as having a positive impact on elder abuse services. To facilitate this positive impact, practitioners need to be aware of legislation and existing protocols between agencies; to improve existing protocols, as necessary; and to establish protocols where there are none.

Recommendations to State Courts

The last article focuses on developing knowledge about judicial handling of elder abuse cases and using that knowledge to develop recommended guidelines to help courts. Twenty-nine recommendations are made as to ways that State courts can improve their handling of elder abuse cases, ensure that these cases enter the court system, and coordinate the judicial system with other community resources. Specific recommendations include:

- Providing training on elder abuse issues for judges.

- Making courts more flexible to accommodate the special needs of the elderly.

- Encouraging the formation or continuation of multidisciplinary, interagency task forces on elder abuse.

- Including elder abuse experts on court advisory councils.

- Making victim/witness advocates or other court staff available to help victims throughout the court process in both criminal and civil proceedings.

Coordination and Collaboration

Findings and Implications Drawn From

Working Relationships Between Adult Protective Services, Aging Agencies, and Law Enforcement Agencies— A Short-Term Project

by Toshio Tatara and Margaret Rittman[1]

Purpose of Research

To examine the nature of the working relationships that State adult protective service (APS) units and State units on aging have with law enforcement agencies in handling domestic and institutional elder abuse cases; to obtain information about formal protocols or agreements that State and/or local aging and APS units have with law enforcement agencies; and to obtain information about joint training, research, or public education programs.

Methods

Beginning in August 1991, survey questionnaires were sent to the APS and aging agencies in each of the States, two territories, and the District of Columbia. Agencies in 45 of these jurisdictions returned completed forms.

Findings

Results from the survey questionnaires were analyzed from two perspectives: domestic elder abuse and institutional elder abuse.

The survey on domestic elder abuse revealed:

- The majority of States (36 of 45 jurisdictions) have laws mandating law enforcement involvement in handling domestic elder abuse cases (e.g., investigations and home visits for evidence gathering).

- The law enforcement agencies most often required to be involved are the police (22 of 45), local prosecutor (21), sheriff (20), and court (18). One or more responding jurisdictions require involvement by the State's attorney, attorney general, district attorney, coroner, county protective services, and county probation officers.

- Few States (3 of 45) have formal protocols between State APS or aging agencies and State law enforcement; local protocols are somewhat more common (14 of 45), but still relatively rare.

- Regardless of whether or not formal protocols exist between APS/aging and law enforcement agencies, in the majority of States, these agencies regularly work together (31 of 45) and undertake joint training, public education, and research activities (31 of 45). Law enforcement agencies or officials most likely to participate in joint activities are the police, the sheriff, the attorney general, medicaid fraud control unit, court, and the district attorney.

The survey on institutional elder abuse revealed:

- The majority of States (32 of 45) have laws mandating law enforcement involvement in handling institutional elder abuse cases.

- Law enforcement agencies or officials most frequently required to be involved are police (17 of 45), local prosecutor (17), sheriff (14),

---

[1] From a Final Report, National Aging Resource Center on Elder Abuse (NARCEA), April 1992.

and court (10). One or more States require involvement of the attorney general, State's attorney, county protective services unit, coroner, and medicaid fraud control unit.

- Formal protocols are rare at both the State level (9 of 45) and the local level (4).

- In about half the States, law enforcement works with APS/aging agencies (23 of 45) and participates with them in other activities (21).

- In about half the States, law enforcement works with APS/aging agencies (23 of 45) and participates with them in other activities (21).

Implications for Law Enforcement*

The following conclusions were drawn:

- Law enforcement officials should be aware of existing legislation mandating their involvement with APS/aging agencies and protocols for implementing such involvement.

- Where protocols do not exist or where they are ineffective, law enforcement officials should work with APS/aging agencies to establish or improve such protocols.

Selected Findings and Implications Drawn From

Collaboration Between Protective Services and Law Enforcement: The Massachusetts Model

by Donna M. Reulbach and Jane Tewksbury[2]

Purpose of Research

To develop, test, and refine interagency protocols regarding elder abuse, neglect, and financial exploitation; improve communication and flow of information between the protective services agency and law enforcement; increase cross-agency referrals; and facilitate development of service plans to support victims throughout the criminal justice process.

Methods

The development of the Middlesex County Guidelines for Handling Elder Abuse Referrals was a collaborative effort of Massachusetts Protective Services and the Middlesex County District Attorney's Office. This collaborative effort involved reviewing cases referred to the district attorney and examining their outcome in terms of satisfaction of the district attorney, the protective services agency, and the victim; agreeing upon common language, terms, and concepts; cross-training of both front-line and supervisory police, and prosecutorial, victim/witness, and protective service personnel about the requirements and implications of mandatory reporting; and developing and testing guidelines focusing on mandatory reporting requirements of statutes and regulations.

Findings

Historically, there has been considerable mistrust and little cooperation between the social services and criminal justice systems. The study results showed:

- Despite statutory mandatory reporting requirements, protective services personnel often failed to report elder abuse and neglect to the district attorney. Many protective services workers believed that such reports would

---

* These implications are not explicit in the report but appear evident from the survey results.

[2] From the *Journal of Elder Abuse & Neglect*, 6(2) (1994), 9–21.

necessarily result in criminal prosecution and probably incarceration of the perpetrator/caregiver. In fact, however, not all reports resulted in criminal prosecution and not all prosecutions resulted in incarceration. Moreover, inadequate reporting by protective services personnel often resulted in lost or destroyed physical evidence.

- When protective services did refer cases to the district attorney's office, there was often inadequate followup by either side, that is:
  — The district attorney's office often failed to investigate to see if criminal charges could be brought.
  — Protective services rarely requested to be kept apprised of how the prosecutor's office was going to proceed—information that was critical to the development of an appropriate service plan for the victim.

- Despite statutory mandatory requirements that police report elder abuse and neglect to the protective services agency, police rarely did so. Consequently, protective services was unable to provide needed services to victims, initiate alternative interventions when criminal prosecutions would not go forth, or develop victim safety plans to support victims through the criminal justice process.

Conclusions

Based on case reviews, interagency guidelines were developed, field-tested, and—after extensive cross-training of Protective Services and law enforcement staff—implemented. From this process researchers concluded:

- A coordinated multidisciplinary effort to develop and implement interagency protocols can increase case referral, improve interagency communication, and result in better investigations and more timely prosecutions.

- The development and cultivation of personal contacts among all of the involved agencies is an essential ingredient of effective interagency cooperation and collaboration.

- Protocols would:
  — Clearly define the types of cases protective services should refer to the prosecutor.
  — Specify who on the prosecutorial staff is to receive referrals.
  — Detail the steps the prosecutor's office should take upon receiving such referrals, emphasizing timeliness.
  — Specify the types of information protective services and prosecutors should share with each other.

- The process of developing protocols can also result in the identification of statutory or regulatory obstacles to interagency cooperation. For example, in addition to developing the Guidelines, the project's collaborators:
  — Drafted and filed with the legislature a criminal neglect bill.
  — Successfully sought an amendment of protective services legislation to include financial exploitation as a reportable condition.
  — Obtained modification of protective services requirements so as to allow law enforcement to assume early and exclusive jurisdiction in investigating cases involving the death of the victim.

Implications for Law Enforcement and Prosecutors

Experience with the Massachusetts model resulted in several recommendations to improve the response to elder abuse and neglect cases:

- Supervisory and front-line personnel in the police department, prosecutor's office, and the protective services agency should participate in and coordinate their agency's efforts.

- Police should report elder abuse, neglect, and financial exploitation to the protective services agency.

- Prosecutors should keep the protective services agency advised about how specific cases are proceeding so that it can:

  — Deliver needed services to victims.

  — Arrange for alternative interventions to protect victims when prosecution will not go forth.

  — Develop victim safety plans to support victims through the criminal justice process when prosecution will go forth.

- Prosecutors should maintain close coordination with protective services to:

  — Clarify whether or not specific cases should be referred to the prosecutor and what the procedure is for handling cases referred by protective services.

  — Encourage reporting of elderly abuse cases that might warrant criminal prosecution.

  — Obtain assistance in securing information or testimony from intimidated victims.

  — Obtain useful information about the facts and circumstances of the reported prosecutorial handling of specific cases.

- The prosecutorial screening function should be centralized and should encourage consultation with protective services workers who are unsure about the suitability of referral in specific cases. Screeners can also serve as troubleshooters to field complaints from protective services about prosecutorial handling of specific cases. The prosecutor should encourage protective services to establish a parallel position to field complaints from prosecutors.

Recommendations to State Courts

Selected Findings and Implications Drawn From

Recommended Guidelines for State Courts Handling Cases Involving Elder Abuse

by Lori A. Stiegel[3]

Purpose of Research

To develop a base of knowledge about judicial handling of cases involving elder abuse and to use that knowledge to develop recommended guidelines to help courts provide judicial solutions that respect the values and wishes of elder abuse victims while protecting their welfare; ease access of appropriate cases to the court system; and enhance coordination among the court system and public and private agencies serving abused elders.

Methods

The project involved: (1) review and analysis of relevant civil and criminal statutes, case law, and legal and social sciences literature; (2) two Delphi consensus-building surveys completed by 214 and 170 respondents, respectively, including judges, court administrators, legal services, private attorneys, prosecutors, adult protective services and social services personnel, staff from Medicaid fraud control units and State attorney's general offices, health care providers, long-term care ombudsman program staff, researchers, and victim/witness advocates; (3) development, expert advisory committee review, and revision of draft recommendations based on survey issues that elicited at least 75 percent "consensus"; and (4) continual review of proposed recommendations by nine focus groups representing relevant national organizations.

Findings

Criminal court involvement in elder abuse cases is appropriate when:

- The case involves criminal intent, criminal neglect, or a crime committed in a nursing home that would be prosecuted if committed on the street.

- The alleged offender is a public guardian, a person with a history of abusive behavior, a caregiver, or someone who violated protective orders.

- The abused elder is mentally ill or mentally impaired.

- The abuse involved severe physical harm or injury or sexual abuse.

Noncriminal court involvement in elder abuse cases is appropriate when:

- The case involves abandonment, domestic violence, fiduciary abuse, elder abuse within a Medicaid-certified nursing facility; emotional, psychological, or mental abuse; financial exploitation; improper institutionalization; sexual abuse; theft by a caregiver; or severe harm or death.

- The alleged abuser is a guardian or caregiver.

- A protective order or injunction is needed to stop the abuse.

- An incapacitated older person refuses to accept protective services.

---

[3] From a publication of the American Bar Association Commission on Legal Problems of the Elderly, developed under State Justice Institute grant #SJI–93–12J–E–274, 1995.

Barriers inhibiting entry of elder abuse cases into the courts include certain concerns or beliefs of abused elders such as:

- Reluctance to get family members or caretakers in trouble.
- Dependence on abusers for companionship or care.
- Fear that court involvement will result in their removal from the home.
- Fear of testifying and shame in airing their abuse in court.
- Lack of knowledge about legal remedies.
- Logistical problems in getting to and spending time in court.
- Belief that court intervention will not prevent further abuse or retaliation.

Barriers inhibiting entry of elder abuse cases into the courts include certain institutional barriers such as:

- Judges' insensitivity and ignorance about elder abuse, which inhibits lawyers, prosecutors, and abused persons from bringing cases.
- Court delays that result in elders' forgetting about the abuse or in the lessening of their ability to recall information about it.
- Lack of knowledge by prosecutors, lawyers, and law enforcement officers about handling elder abuse cases.
- Lack of coordination between adult protective service workers and law enforcement.

Implications for Judges

The project developed a total of 29 recommendations on ways State courts can improve their handling of elder abuse cases, ensure that elder abuse cases enter the court system, and coordinate the judicial system functions with that of other community resources. Among these:

- Judges should be trained about the dynamics of elder abuse and family violence, relevant laws, available services for elder abuse victims, and effective handling of elder abuse cases. Training should include cross-training with other relevant professionals.
- In handling elder abuse cases, judges should make accommodations for victims with physical and mental deficiencies, be flexible in scheduling hearings to accommodate needs of elderly victims, and expedite cases.
- If the capacity of elder abuse victims is an issue, judges should use experts trained and knowledgeable about the problems of older persons to assess capacity. In noncriminal proceedings involving incapacitated victims, judges should use guardians and alternatives to guardianship appropriately and ensure that, when one is to be used, an appointed counsel is assigned as early as possible. In criminal proceedings involving incapacitated victims, judges should allow prosecutors special latitude in questioning victims, and ensure that plea negotiations and sentences meet the victims' needs.
- Courts should establish intracourt communication systems to ensure that judges hearing elder abuse cases are aware of related cases that have been previously heard or are underway in different divisions.
- Judges should encourage the formation or continuation of multidisciplinary, interagency task forces on elder abuse, and have elder abuse experts serve on court advisory councils.

Implications for Victim/Witness Advocates and Court Staff

Victim/witness advocates or other court staff should assist older abused persons throughout the court process in both criminal and noncriminal proceedings.

Victim/witness advocates need to learn about the dynamics of elder abuse, the jurisdiction's adult protective services, and resources offered by other network services for the elderly.

Chapter Three: Research on Legal Interventions in Domestic Violence Cases

As public awareness about the prevalence and nature of spouse and partner violence has increased, so too has public demand that the justice system step in to stop the violence, rather than continue to treat it as a private matter between consenting adults. Accordingly, police, prosecutors, probation officers, and judges are using or adapting various strategies to this end. Researchers have examined some of these strategies, including civil protection orders, arrest and prosecution, and court-ordered treatment of offenders. At the same time, research has shed increasing light on characteristics common to batterers.[1]

Batterer Characteristics

Justice system practitioners must have at least a general understanding of the nature of batterers to be able to deal with them effectively and to protect their victims from further violence. Two of the studies summarized in this chapter specifically sought to identify characteristics predictive of domestic violence. Although their methods differ considerably, both conclude that criminal history, history of mental illness, and use of alcohol and drugs are among the common characteristics of batterers. (These and other batterer characteristics are also included among the findings of several other studies summarized in this chapter under other headings.)

Civil Protection Orders

Restraining orders have been touted as workable and preferable alternatives to criminal proceedings or useful tools in conjunction with criminal proceedings in domestic violence cases. They also have been criticized as ineffective or, worse, as providing false comfort to victims who rely on them.

The four studies on civil protection orders explore the benefits and limitations of issuing and enforcing such orders, assess their impact in reducing abusive behavior and improving the quality of women's lives, and provide some insight into abusers against whom restraining orders are issued and their future risk of abuse. Generally, the studies find that civil protection orders have important, but limited, value to victims. Restraining orders can provide immediate relief from the violence and enhance victims' self-esteem. However, they are rarely effective in reducing future violence unless accompanied by safety planning and other community services,[2] or when, as is commonly

---

[1] In 1997, the U.S. Department of Justice's Violence Against Women Grants Office (VAWGO) launched an initiative to identify and develop promising practices for law enforcement, prosecution, the courts, and victim services. Findings from expert panels, a national survey of hundreds of practitioners, and indepth interviews with practitioners will be published in the spring of 1998 as a manual to help States and subgrantees with Federal Violence Against Women Act funds draw on the most promising practices in their fields. In the meantime, VAWGO has released a document entitled "Assessing Justice System Response to Violence Against Women" that contains checklists for each discipline, supplemented by selected program profiles. It is available on the VAWGO Web page (http://www.vaw.umn.edu), or by calling 800–256–5883.

[2] Many advocacy groups, including the American Bar Association Commission on Domestic Violence, recommend that safety planning be conducted regularly with all victims of domestic violence. The Commission also recommends the development of "one-stop shopping" for victim services or intake centers in courts, at shelters, or at police stations.

the case, the batterers have a history of severe violence or are substance abusers. Not surprisingly, protection orders also have been found to be ineffective when not promptly served or effectively enforced on the abuser. Given the limitations of civil protection orders, several of the studies recommend that domestic violence cases be prosecuted as well, and one study recommends that prosecution be "no drop."[3]

Arrest

One of the most widely implemented—but controversial—efforts to deal with domestic violence in recent years has been the adoption of proarrest or mandatory arrest policies.[4] Some believe such policies are necessary to convince batterers that, regardless of the relationship between the parties, violence is a crime. Others believe proarrest policies only confirm victims' sense of powerlessness over their own lives. The research projects described show how the numerous variables associated with arresting batterers can complicate the evaluation of these policies, and lead to some different conclusions. Generally, however, the studies find that mandatory arrest as a deterrent to future violence works better for some perpetrators than for others, and that it is more effective in the short term than in the long run. Several also argue that deterrence should not be the only value on which mandatory arrest is judged.

Prosecution

The prosecution studies described in this volume shed light on various aspects of prosecuting domestic violence cases. The first study concerns a survey of how these cases are handled in large jurisdictions, that is, what sort of domestic violence cases prosecutors handle, how cases come into the office, and how they are dealt with in terms of pretrial release, postcharge diversion, trial, and sentencing. The next study examines the effectiveness of eight combinations of arrest and prosecution policies—including a "no drop" option—in reducing renewed violence. It concludes that victim involvement in decisionmaking can reduce the likelihood of rebattering. Several others address evidence about battering—how it differs from "the battered woman syndrome," how it should and should not be used for defense or prosecution purposes, and current trends in statutes and court decisions that recognize the validity of such evidence to supplement, but not to supplant, more traditional forms of evidence.

Court-Ordered Treatment

Two studies summarized in this chapter address the effectiveness of court-ordered treatment for reducing renewed violence by batterers. One concludes that batterer treatment does not reduce the prevalence or frequency of violence, while the other finds that integrated substance abuse/batterer treatment programs are more effective in reducing battering than separate treatment programs for battering and substance abuse.

Other

Finally, this section of the publication includes a study summary relating to the corporate-sector response to domestic violence.

---

[3] In 1997, the American Bar Association adopted a resolution recognizing that "no drop" prosecutions can be very helpful in sparing victims from the sole responsibility for prosecuting their batterers but at the same time urging that such prosecutions be undertaken with great care to ensure victims' protection.

[4] The Federal Violence Against Women Act of 1994 encourages police departments to adopt either proarrest or mandatory arrest policies (42 U.S.C. 3796hh(b)(1) and (c)(1)). The American Bar Association has endorsed the adoption of proarrest policies (February 1997).

Batterer and Victim Characteristics

Selected Findings and Implications Drawn From

Findings About Partner Violence From the Dunedin Multidisciplinary Health and Development Study

by Terrie E. Moffitt, Avshalom Caspi, and Phil A. Silva[5]

Purpose of Research

To study the health and development of a complete cohort of infants born between April 1, 1972, and March 31, 1973, in Dunedin on New Zealand's South Island. The goal was to improve prediction, understanding, and treatment of partner violence by studying the developmental experiences, personal characteristics, and situational circumstances that lead individuals into partner violence, and to help make policy to deter batterers through arrest, prosecution, or therapy.

Methods

This research summary is part of the Dunedin Multidisciplinary Health and Development Study, a 21-year study of a representative birth cohort. The cohort was assessed at ages 3, 5, 7, 9, 11, 13, 15, 18, and 21. When the cohort became 21 years old, the researchers embedded questions about partner violence in a 50-minute standardized interview about intimate relationships.

Findings

The section of the study on partner violence found that partner violence is strongly associated with the following:

- Cohabitation at a young age.
- A variety of mental illnesses.
- A background of family adversity, leaving school early, and juvenile aggression.
- Conviction for other types of crime, especially violent crime.
- Drug abuse.
- Long-term unemployment.
- Motherhood at a young age.

Implications for the Criminal Justice System

Based on the study results, the researchers concluded:

- Perpetrators of partner violence tend to be perpetrators of other violent crimes. This finding may point to a need to coordinate policing and judicial approaches to batterers.

---

[5] The Dunedin Multidisciplinary Health and Development Research Unit is supported by the New Zealand Health Research Council. This research was supported by grant #94–IJ–CX–0041 from the National Institute of Justice. Additional support was provided by U.S. Public Health Service (USPHS) grant MH–45070 to Terrie E. Moffitt from the Violence and Traumatic Stress Research Branch of the National Institute of Mental Health, by USPHS grant MH–49414 to Avshalom Caspi from the Personality and Social Processes Branch of the National Institute of Mental Health, by the William T. Grant Foundation, and by the William Freeman Vilas Trust at the University of Wisconsin. Forthcoming in 1998.

- Interventions should target teen mothers, to protect very young children from high rates of exposure to family violence.

- Domestic violence should be a standard intake assessment in all public mental health settings, to identify both perpetrators and victims before injury brings them in contact with medical practitioners.

Selected Findings and Implications Drawn From

Florida Mortality Review Project: Executive Summary

by Byron Johnson, De Li, and Neil Websdale[6]

Purpose of Research

To construct "red flags" that might serve as bases to intervene and prevent domestic fatalities.

Methods

Data sources included police records; court documents; autopsy reports; newspaper accounts; hospital reports; and interviews with police, court personnel, mental health workers, social service providers, and advocates for battered women. Data were gathered on victim and perpetrator characteristics, including gender, race, and relationship; "situational antecedents" such as prior history of domestic violence, emotional or mental difficulties, and acknowledged conflict in the relationship; and the incident itself, including mode of killing, presence of other parties at the scene, nonfatal wounding of others, and use of weapons, drugs, or alcohol.

While acknowledging the potential objection that the many variables of domestic fatalities are inseparable and interwoven parts of an abusive relationship, the researchers contend that breaking down the various components allows for a determination of combinations of subcomponents most likely associated with, and therefore predictive of, lethal domestic situations.

Findings

Data sources revealed:

- Domestic fatalities for 1994 were underreported by the Florida Department of Law Enforcement. Whereas the official count was 230, the study revealed 321 domestic fatalities, 281 of which were consistent with the Florida domestic violence statute. Forty-seven of these domestic fatalities were suicides within homicide-suicide incidents.[7]

---

[6] From research undertaken by the Center for Justice Research and Education at Lamar University (Texas) for the Florida Governor's Task Force on Domestic and Sexual Violence; funded by grant #95–WF–NX–0012 from the Stop Violence Against Women program, Bureau of Justice Assistance, U.S. Department of Justice. For further information, contact Robin Hassler, Executive Director, Governor's Task Force on Domestic and Sexual Violence, 2555 Shumard Boulevard, Tallahassee, Florida 32399–2100.

[7] These figures continue to be updated as new data (e.g., cases solved) and access to additional data sources (e.g., child and protective services case files) are obtained.

- Of domestic homicide victims, nearly 95 percent of the women were killed by men, while only a quarter of the men were killed by women.
- Domestic fatalities involving female victims were usually final events in long-standing abusive relationships; this was not the case when the victims were male.
- Women who killed men usually did so out of self-defense or, less often, the defense of their children.
- The rate of domestic homicides perpetrated by women is considerably higher for blacks than for whites or Latinos; the rate was lowest for Latinos.
- Deaths of children resulting from abuse and/or neglect showed a strong correlation with unmarried caretakers, poverty, and a history of physical abuse.
- "Red flags" identified with the 1994 domestic fatalities in Florida were as follows:
  — Prior history of domestic violence in the relationship.
  — Obsessive-possessive beliefs on the part of the perpetrator, that is, a perpetrator's belief or sense of possession and total control over the victim.
  — Threats to kill.
  — Perpetrator belief of betrayal by partner, or morbid jealousy, including departure from expected role.
  — Victim attempts to break away.
  — Prior police calls to the residence.
  — Drug and/or alcohol use prior to the incident.
  — Prior criminal histories of victims and perpetrators.
  — History of mental illness or medical treatment of mental health problems.

Implications for Law Enforcement

Since prior police contact is a "red flag," it is critical that police document the nature of their involvement with domestic violence incidents. Such information can be used to screen high-risk cases. Police reports should contain the following information:

- The names of the victims.
- History of prior violence.
- Police involvement, injunctions, and prior criminal histories.
- History of possessive beliefs, mental illness, and so forth.

Police could receive sensitivity training on the importance and implications of the "red flags,"* including:

- Threats to kill an intimate partner or spouse, which need to be taken seriously.
- Complaints from individuals who have obtained injunctions, left the household, or previously summoned the police, which need to be given priority attention.*

Police could work with judicial and social services groups to develop plans for unusual and highly proactive interventions.

---

* These implications are not explicit in the executive summary but appear to follow from the findings.

Implications for Judges

To improve their role in domestic violence interventions and thus prevent fatalities, judges could:

- Be made aware of the existence and nature of "red flags" for domestic fatalities and take them into consideration in fashioning specific conditions in restraining orders and sentences.*

- Encourage recipients to develop safety plans and work with local domestic violence agencies when issuing protective orders.*

- Work with police and social services groups to develop plans for unusual and highly proactive interventions.

---

* These implications are not explicit in the executive summary but appear to follow from the findings.

Civil Protection Orders

Selected Findings and Implications Drawn From

Civil Protection Orders: Legislation, Current Court Practice, and Enforcement

by Peter Finn and Sarah Colson[8]

Purpose of Research

To explore concerns involved in issuing and enforcing civil protection orders.

Methods

Information was drawn from four sources: (1) a review of pertinent State statutes and case law; (2) telephone interviews with 12 judges and 12 victim advocates; (3) examination of program documentation in Duluth, Minnesota, and Seattle, Washington; (4) site visits to Portland, Maine; Portland, Oregon; Springfield, Illinois; Chicago, Illinois; Nashville, Tennessee; Philadelphia, Pennsylvania; and Colorado Springs, Colorado, which included personal interviews with judges, prosecutors, law enforcement officers, women's advocates, and battered women; courtroom observation; and—in two of the sites—ride-alongs with police officers.

Findings

Civil protection orders can provide:

- A workable alternative to criminal charges or an additional remedy for many victims seeking protection from further domestic abuse.

- Immediate relief to domestic violence victims.

- An alternative form of relief where the level of evidence may not sustain criminal charges or where the victim, for reasons of age, illness, or alcohol or drug dependency, may be a weak prosecution witness.

The utility of protection orders may depend on their specificity, consistency of enforcement, and the ease with which they are obtained. Serious limitations of civil protection orders include:

- Widespread lack of enforcement, even though such orders allow for expansion of police arrest powers and increase the ability of police to monitor repeat offenders.

---

[8] From an Issues and Practices Report prepared for the National Institute of Justice by Abt Associates Inc., Contract #OJP–86–C–002, published by the National Institute of Justice, March 1990, NCJ 123263. Since this groundbreaking study was published in 1990, there have been a number of changes regarding the issuance of protection orders, some likely as a result of the problems flagged in the report. For example, many jurisdictions now provide 24-hour access to protection orders and improved court forms or computerized filing and petition procedures. Many States have enacted statutes making violations of protection orders a matter of criminal contempt, a misdemeanor, or even a felony. Federal law now makes mutual protection orders issued in violation of due process unenforceable and prohibits abusers convicted of domestic violence or having outstanding protection orders against them from possessing firearms. Finally, increased emphasis has been placed on substantive criminal prosecutions of domestic violence.

- Uncertainty about enforcement of the orders on the part of both police and judges.
- Common statutory weaknesses, including:
  — Filing fees.
  — Lack of procedures and funds for training and supervising clerks to assist petitioners seeking protection orders.
  — Narrow eligibility categories.
  — Lack of means of issuing emergency orders when courts are not in session.
  — Requirement of service to the defendant before the order becomes effective, leaving victims unprotected until service has been made.
  — Failure to provide for case tracking to determine compliance.
  — Failure to provide law enforcement officers with adequate authorization for arresting respondents who violate protection orders by designating violations as civil (rather than criminal) contempt or misdemeanors or by failing to provide for warrantless arrest for violations.
- Petition procedures that require the assistance of counsel. Even with a simplified petitioning procedure and energetic lay assistance, victims not represented by counsel are less likely to get protection orders. If an order is issued, it is less likely to contain all appropriate provisions regarding exclusion from the residence, temporary custody of children, child support, and protective limitations on visitation rights.

Centralized court administration of domestic violence petitions reduces postponements of hearings due to attorney absences and helps judges develop specialized expertise in domestic violence cases. It also facilitates matters for victims. On the other hand, full-time work on domestic violence cases can be exhausting and "burnout" is likely.

Implications for Judges

The researchers offer several recommendations or points of consideration to address concerns regarding civil protection orders and to improve judges' effectiveness in issuing and enforcing such orders. These recommendations are in the areas of guideline development and court policies, victims' access to the petitioning process, information on the victims' circumstances, and education about civil protection orders and domestic abuse.

Guideline development. Judges can develop guidelines for when to issue and how to enforce civil protection orders based on statutory authorization, available case law, and local court procedures.

Guidelines for *issuing* civil protection orders should:

- Ensure that such orders take into account a wide range of behaviors by abusers.
- Include all statutorily authorized protections to meet the needs and circumstances of the victims they are intended to protect.
- Include other appropriate forms of relief, which might include eviction of the offender from the family home, no-contact provisions, denial of or limitations on child custody and visitation by the offender, and mandatory counseling for batterers.

To address other concerns regarding issuing protection orders, judges can:

- Have clearly defined procedures for notice and hearing to address concerns about defendants' due process rights in protection order proceedings.
- Make protection orders as specific as possible so as to minimize doubt by victims, respondents, law enforcement officials, and other judges about abusers' proscribed behavior.

Guidelines for *enforcing* civil protection orders should:

- Clarify what procedures law enforcement officers are statutorily required and authorized to follow and what procedures judges themselves will follow in holding violation hearings.

- Address distinctions between civil and criminal contempt as well as probable cause requirements for warrantless arrests in connection with violation of protection orders.

- Address defendants' due process rights in enforcement proceedings and sentencing considerations.

Even where statutory weaknesses exist, judges can establish a court policy on enforcement of orders that includes:

- Admonishing defendants.

- Establishing procedures for modifying orders.

- Promoting—as appropriate—the arrest of violators.

- Handling violators sternly.

Judges should also ensure that law enforcement officers know that prompt service of protection orders on respondents is a top priority.

Victims' access. Judges can play a key role in promoting victims' access to counsel or the petitioning process, even where not explicitly mandated or authorized by statute. Judges can:

- Encourage local legal aid organizations, bar association pro bono projects, and law school clinical programs to place a high priority on representing victim petitioners.

- Provide training for victim advocates and meet regularly with victim advocacy groups to address mutual problems and preview changes in court procedures.

- Help train court clerks to improve their assistance to petitioners, including:

  — Ensuring that clerks have written instructions for assessing petitioners' eligibility for protection orders under the State statute.

  — Providing firm instructions not to assess petitioners' credibility.

  — Advising them what course of action to follow or giving legal advice.

In addition, courts can assist victims who cannot secure legal counsel or who prefer to proceed without counsel by providing simplified forms and clerical assistance to help with the writing and filing of petitions. Judges can ask questions of petitioners about what assistance is needed (e.g., child support or alternative living arrangements) and about other matters that should be taken into account, such as potential danger to children.

Information on victims' circumstances. Even when judges are not statutorily required to hold a hearing prior to issuing a temporary protection order, they may find it of value to inform themselves about the victim's circumstances. Judges could:

- Speak with the petitioner to determine what dangers may exist and, accordingly, what provisions need to be in the protection order to ensure the safety of the petitioner and other members of the petitioner's household.

- Inform the petitioner of the importance of appearing for the hearing on a permanent order, and assess the petitioner's credibility and thus safeguard the rights of the defendant.

Judges may also find it valuable to gather information on the victim prior to allowing dismissal of a temporary order or dismissing the proceedings for a permanent order because of the petitioner's failure to appear. Judges may wish to inquire as to whether the petitioner has been intimidated or has failed to understand the necessity of appearing at the hearing for the permanent order.

Education about domestic abuse. Judges need to:

- Be aware of the cyclical nature of domestic violence, whereby incidents of abuse are followed by periods of affectionate behavior and promises to reform. Judges may find this knowledge useful when faced with repeat petitioners. Even several temporary emergency petitions followed by failure to pursue petitions for permanent orders do not necessarily imply bad faith on the part of the petitioner nor suggest that successive emergency orders are not warranted.

- Understand and not underestimate the power of judicial admonitions in promoting abusers' adherence to the requirements of protective orders.

Training on civil protection orders. Judicial training in this area should include:

- A thorough analysis of the State statute.

- An explanation of how civil protection orders can contribute to maintaining law and order.

- An explanation of the dynamics of battering and the psychosocial and institutional factors that sustain it.

- A discussion of how judges can best use their authority in the courtroom to intervene effectively in domestic violence situations.

Implications for Law Enforcement

Training on civil protection orders would help police officers:

- Provide victims with information about the protection order process, which they are often required to do by statute or by police department general orders.

- Become aware that quick service of protection orders is important to prevent renewed violence.

- Learn of the statutory requirements regarding enforcement of protective orders, police liability for failure to enforce, and the advantages of strict enforcement for police officers.

Implications for Prosecutors

Whether or not the State statute mandates assistance to victims seeking protection orders, prosecutors may provide that assistance as part of a larger mandate to control crime. Because protection orders offer an opportunity to prevent future crime and enhance law enforcement, regular involvement by prosecutors, while creating an immediate time demand, may be viewed as a desirable investment in reducing future caseloads.

Implications for Victim Advocates

Victim advocates can assist petitioners in various ways, including:

- Determining their eligibility under the statute to petition for an order.

- Explaining the protection order process and assisting in filling out forms.

- Explaining the legal help available, relief that can be requested, and the limitations of an order.

- Accompanying petitioners to the initial hearing for a temporary order.

- Helping prepare petitioners for the hearing for the full order.

- Accompanying petitioners to the hearing for a permanent order.

Victim advocates can also expedite court proceedings by performing the following functions:

- Prescreening petitioners for eligibility criteria under the statute and making sure that petition forms are properly completed before the hearing.

- Accompanying victims in the courtroom, resulting in more orderly proceedings.

- Arranging for witnesses to appear with the victim, facilitating complete presentation of evidence.

- Addressing petitioners' fears about appearing for the hearing for the permanent order.

- Increasing the court's ability to provide needed protection.

- Helping to identify cases in which attorney assistance is essential.

Selected Findings and Implications Drawn From

The Effectiveness of Civil Protection Orders

by Susan Keilitz, Paula Hannaford, and Hillery S. Efkeman[9]

Purpose of Research

To measure how various factors affect the effectiveness of civil protection orders in terms of improving the quality of women's lives and of deterring abusive behavior. These factors include the court intake process, the level of assistance available to petitioners, the level of abuse the victim suffered, and the criminal history of the respondent.

Methods

The study examined civil protection orders in the Family Court in Wilmington, Delaware; the County Court in Denver, Colorado; and the District of Columbia Superior Court. Data were compiled from initial telephone interviews with 285 women petitioners approximately a month after they received a protection order; followup interviews with 177 of these women about 6 months later; civil case records of petitioners participating in the study; and criminal history records of men named in the protection orders the study participants obtained.

Findings

Data from interviews and criminal and court records disclosed:

- Most of the petitioners had suffered physical abuse, and for more than half the physical abuse was severe. Few victims sought protection orders immediately; a quarter had endured the abuse for more than 5 years.

- The longer the women experienced abuse, the more intense the abusive behavior became.

- The majority of abusers had criminal records, and most had been arrested for violent crimes other than domestic violence.

- Temporary protection orders can be useful even if the victim does not follow through to obtain a permanent order. Victims' most common stated reason for not returning for a permanent protection order was that their abusers had stopped bothering them.

- While respondents usually violate protective orders in some way, the orders generally

---

[9] From *Civil Protection Orders: The Benefits and Limitations for Victims of Domestic Violence*, an Executive Summary of a National Center for State Courts study funded by the National Institute of Justice under grant #93–IJ–CX–0035, 1997, NCJ 164866.

deter repeated incidents of physical and psychological abuse.

- While victims whose partners have a history of violent crime are more likely than other victims to be revictimized after receiving protection orders, they are also more likely than other victims with protection orders to believe that the orders have improved their well-being in terms of self-esteem and feelings of security.

- Victims do not use the contempt process to enforce orders.

- The potential for linking victims to services through the court process has not been achieved.

Implications for all Criminal Justice Practitioners

To improve the level of assistance, practitioners, including victim advocates, need to:

- Provide counseling to domestic violence victims as soon as possible about the low likelihood of abatement of the abuse without a specific intervention. In cases where the abuser has a criminal history/record of violence, the dual interventions of criminal prosecution and civil protection orders may best meet the victim's objective need for increased protection and subjective need for self-esteem and greater feelings of security.

- Stress the importance of safety planning to victims seeking protection orders, particularly those whose abusers have a history of violent crime.

Implications for Prosecutors

Since protection orders are less likely to deter abusers with a history of violent crime than other abusers, criminal prosecution may be required to curb their abusive behavior.

Implications for Judges and Court Employees

Issuing protection orders can provide the necessary intervention to abate the increasing intensity of domestic violence. Protection orders should take into account:

- The particular needs of the petitioner. Among the potential orders issued should be exclusive use of the family residence by the victim and substance abuse treatment and batterer treatment for the abuser.

- The criminal history of alleged abusers. This is critical because abusers with a history of violent and drug- and alcohol-related crimes engage in particularly intense abuse of their partners. Special conditions such as batterer treatment and substance abuse treatment may be warranted in such cases. In addition, judges should stress to these victims the need for safety precautions and inform them about using law enforcement and the court to enforce the protection orders.

To increase the victims' use of the legal system in deterring further violence in their lives, judges can help ensure the provision of the following:

- Education for petitioners about temporary protection orders and about safety planning. This information is critical because significant numbers of victims who have obtained temporary protection orders do not follow through with a request for permanent protection orders.

- User-friendly information to victims who have obtained protection orders about using law enforcement and the contempt process to enforce the orders locally, throughout the State, and in other States.

- User-friendly information for petitioners of protection orders about the full range of special conditions in protection orders and about available services, such as police and prosecutor victim assistance units, victim counseling, shelters for battered women and their children, pro bono legal services, and employment and education counseling.

- A more centralized court process and direct assistance to petitioners for protective orders.

Implications for Law Enforcement

Law enforcement agencies can do more to assist prosecutors in developing cases for prosecution, to arrest perpetrators, and to help victims access the civil protection order process, for instance:

- Police can mandate, as an integral component of officer preparation police training in domestic violence, arrest policies with respect to domestic violence, and enforcement procedures.

- Police can provide victims with user-friendly information about the civil protection order process.

Selected Findings and Implications Drawn From

Effects of Restraining Orders on Domestic Violence Victims

by Adele Harrell and Barbara Smith[10]

Purpose of Research

To assess the impact of restraining orders in domestic violence cases by focusing on the extent to which such orders reduce further abuse of women.

Methods

Data were obtained from a sample of 355 temporary restraining orders issued in two jurisdictions in Colorado during the first 9 months of 1991. The cases involved abuse of a female by a male with whom she lived or had lived or with whom she was involved or had been involved in an intimate relationship. Interviews were conducted 3 months after the order with the women and the men named in the complaints. The women were again interviewed a year following the initial order. Additional information was obtained from court and police records.

Findings

Analysis of the data revealed:

- More than half the women had been physically injured during the incident that led them to seek temporary restraining orders.

- Many women thought the temporary restraining order was helpful in documenting that the abuse had occurred, but fewer than half thought the man believed he had to obey the order.

---

[10] From *Do Arrests and Restraining Orders Work?*, edited by Eve S. Buzawa and Carl G. Buzawa, Sage Publications, 1996. The research was supported by the State Justice Institute, grant #SJI–90–12L–E–054.

- Of the women who obtained temporary restraining orders, three-fifths returned to request that the order be made permanent.
- Women gave several reasons for not returning to request permanent orders, among these:
  — Their abusers had stopped bothering them.
  — Their abusers exerted pressure on them to drop their complaints.
  — They feared retaliation if they persisted in their complaints.
  — Problems had been encountered in getting the temporary orders served on the abusers—a prerequisite to the hearing for the permanent order.
- Other significant factors related to whether the women returned to court for a permanent order were age (older women were more likely to return); race/ethnicity (white and Hispanic women were slightly more likely than black women to return); and whether the women gave the police copies of the restraining orders (those who did were more likely than those who did not to return).
- Factors *not* significantly related to the decision to return for a permanent order included education, employment status, children in the home, whether or not the woman lived with the man at the time of the incident, length of the relationship, duration of abuse in the relationship, and severity of the incident described in the complaint.
- The majority (60 percent) of women with temporary restraining orders reported that the orders were violated in the year after they were issued. Nearly a third (29 percent) reported that the violations involved severe violence.
- Severe violence, other forms of physical violence, and threats or property damage occurred as often for women with permanent orders as they did for women without permanent orders. Permanent orders did significantly reduce psychological abuse.
- The severity of the incident described in the complaint did not predict abusive incidents or specific types of abuse during the year following the initial order. However, severity of prior abuse and persistence in prior abuse were significantly related to the severity of abuse in the year after the restraining order.
- The probability of continued abuse increased when the male strongly resisted the orders at the time of the hearing; when the woman seeking the order was living apart from the abuser at the time the order was sought; and when the woman had children.
- The woman's age, employment status, or financial support from the man after the order were not significantly related to postorder abuse.
- When police arrested the abuser during the incident that led to the protection order, the likelihood of severe violence during the following year diminished but the likelihood of other abusive acts was not reduced.
- Men who voiced strong objections to restraining orders were three to four times as likely to violate the orders.

The researchers concluded:

- The majority of women seeking restraining orders had serious complaints of abuse. Protection orders were generally not sought as a form of early intervention but rather as a signal of desperation following extensive problems.

- Information about the persistence and severity of prior abuse (rather than merely about the abuse that precipitated the request for a protection order or the duration of prior abuse) was useful in assessing for potential lethality and in developing safety plans for the abused.

- Although men named in restraining orders continued their abuse, they were less likely to commit acts of serious violence if arrested.

Implications for Law Enforcement

Law enforcement can take several steps to reduce further violence against women:

- Police can reduce the likelihood of severe violence after the order by being helpful at the time of the initial incident.

- Police can reduce the likelihood of severe violence in the year after the incident by making an arrest at the time of the incident.

- Sheriffs can be more resourceful in helping to serve abusers with temporary protection orders.

- Law enforcement should reexamine the appropriateness of police response to violations and institute training and monitoring of enforcement of orders.

Implications for Judges

Judges can increase the impact of restraining orders and make better informed decisions about granting an order and the conditions of an order, specifically, judges need to:

- Be aware of the history of violence between the parties, the presence of children during the violence, and the full extent of the injuries sustained during the incident that led the woman to seek an order of protection.

- Take a leadership role in working with other agencies to help women get their temporary orders served, including educating sheriffs and having probation departments help locate subjects of the orders who might be on probation.

- Include firm and specific statements about the behavioral requirements of the order and the consequences of noncompliance when the abuser voices strenuous objections to the order.

- Include in the temporary order specific prohibitions against the abuser's pressuring the woman to drop the petition.

- "Customize" standardized forms where warranted to include additional orders and make sure that both the abuser and the abused understand the meaning of the various provisions.

- Treat seriously strenuous objections to the orders by the men against whom they are issued.

- Emphasize during the temporary and permanent hearings that women can, and should, return to court to report violations.

Selected Findings and Implications Drawn From

Re-abuse in a Population of Court-Restrained Male Batterers: Why Restraining Orders Don't Work

by Andrew R. Klein[11]

Purpose of Research

To provide insight into the abusers against whom restraining orders are issued and the effect of the orders in terms of new abuse, and to predict future risk of abuse based on the characteristics of the abuse, the victim, the defendant, or the criminal justice system intervention.

Methods

Data were drawn from 663 restraining order cases—every such case in the Quincy (Massachusetts) District Court in 1990 in which the defendant was a male and the victim a current or former spouse or current or former girlfriend, who either cohabited with the abuser or had a child by him. Each abuser was tracked for 2 years to determine further abuse, that is, an arrest for a criminal violation of the order or for a new assault and/or threat, and/or a new restraining order based on a new incident of abuse filed in the Quincy District Court.

Findings

An examination of the restraining order cases showed that:

- Most abusers brought to civil court by their victims had physically assaulted their victims.

- Most abusers had prior criminal histories; the average record length was 13 complaints. More than half had at least one prior record for an alcohol or drug crime (usually drunk driving), and two-fifths had at least one prior complaint for a crime against the person. Most abusers with histories of crimes against the person had been violent with men as well as women.

- Nearly two-fifths of the incidents resulting in restraining orders involved alcohol or drug use by the abuser.

- A significant number of women requesting restraining orders had taken significant steps to protect themselves prior to coming to court, either by divorcing or by physically separating from their abusers.

- While three-quarters of the women who had received temporary restraining orders returned to court for the contested hearing (for the permanent order), nearly half asked the court to drop the order prior to the 1-year termination date.

- Almost half of the abusers reabused their victims within 2 years of the restraining order. The reabuse rate did not differ for those who maintained the orders and those who dropped them.

---

[11] From *Do Arrests and Restraining Orders Work?*, edited by Eve S. Buzawa and Carl G. Buzawa, Sage Publications, 1996.

- Statistically significant predictors for new abuse as measured by a new arrest were age, prior criminal history, and court-ordered "no contact" provisions:
  — Younger abusers reabuse more than older abusers.
  — Abusers with criminal histories reabuse more than abusers without criminal histories.
  — Abusers with longer prior criminal records reabuse regardless of whether or not the orders specify "no contact" with the victims.
- Variables that do *not* predict new abuse include an arrest at the time of the order, the violent or nonviolent nature of the precipitating incident, and the existence of a prior restraining order.

Conclusion

Civil restraining orders do not adequately protect women from further abuse and a primary reliance on such orders must be seriously questioned. Any effectiveness that they have in preventing reabuse comes from their issuance, rather than their maintenance. Accordingly, their optimal use may be in conjunction with vigorous prosecution and significant sanctioning of abusers.

Implications for Law Enforcement

Arrest for domestic violence should be mandatory whether a restraining order is in effect or not.

Implications for Prosecutors

Given the limitations of civil restraining orders and the risk presented by abusers, prosecutors should consider these cases for criminal prosecution. Prosecutors also need to institute a "no-drop" policy.

Implications for Judges

If abusers are allowed to remain in the community, victim safety requires that they receive the same intensity of supervision and scrutiny as the other more serious offenders currently under community-based supervision.

Arrest

Selected Findings and Implications Drawn From

Does Arrest Deter Domestic Violence?

by Janell D. Schmidt and Lawrence W. Sherman[12]

Purpose of Research

To test the deterrent effects of various police responses to domestic violence.

Methods

The original Minneapolis study and replication studies were controlled experiments in which domestic violence misdemeanor cases were assigned one of several possible responses. In Minneapolis and most of the replication studies, the assignment was random (an exception was Metro-Dade where the police had discretion whether to arrest or not); the efficacy of each treatment was measured by interviews with victims and official records.

The six cities selected for the study and the random assignments to possible treatments were as follows:

- Minneapolis (sample size: 314)
    (1) Arrest.
    (2) Sending the suspect away for 8 hours.
    (3) Advising the couple to get help.
- Metro-Dade (sample size: 907)
    (1) Arrest with followup counseling.
    (2) Arrest without followup counseling.
    (3) No arrest with followup counseling.
    (4) No arrest without followup counseling.
- Colorado Springs (sample size: 1,600)
    (1) Arrest with professional counseling.
    (2) Arrest without professional counseling.
    (3) Issuance of an emergency protection order.
- Milwaukee (sample size: 1,200)
    (1) No arrest.
    (2) A 2-hour arrest.
    (3) Arrest with an overnight stay in jail.
- Charlotte (NC) (sample size: 686)
    (1) Arrest.
    (2) Mediation.
    (3) Separation.
    (4) Citation.
- Omaha (sample size: 330)
    (1) Arrest.
    (2) Sending the suspect away for 8 hours.
    (3) Advising the couple to get help.
    (4) Arrest warrants for absent offenders.
    (5) No followup for absent offenders.

---

[12] From *Do Arrests and Restraining Orders Work?*, edited by Eve S. Buzawa and Carl G. Buzawa, Sage Publications, 1996.

Findings

The research undertaken in the six cities revealed:

- Arrests reduced violence by some abusers (e.g., employed abusers; those whose victims were white and Hispanic) and increased it for others (e.g., unemployed abusers, those whose victims were black).
- Arrests may reduce domestic violence in the short run, but may increase it in the long run.
- None of the innovative treatments—namely, counseling or protective orders—produced any improvement over arrest versus no arrest.
- Citations to appear in court caused more violence than arrests. (Charlotte)
- Offenders who had left the scene before the police arrived and against whom warrants were issued were responsible for less repeat violence than absent offenders against whom warrants were not issued. (Omaha)

Implications for Legislators and Law Enforcement

The following recommendations were drawn:

- Legislators should repeal mandatory arrest laws and authorize structured police discretion.
- Legislators should allow police to make warrantless arrests.
- Police should serve warrants on absent offenders.
- Special units and policies should focus on chronically violent individuals.

Implications for Prosecutors

Prosecutors should issue warrants for absent offenders.

Conclusions and Implications Drawn From

Must We Stop Arresting Batterers?: Analysis and Policy Implications of New Police Domestic Violence Studies

by Joan Zorza[13]

Purpose of Research

To review and critique the methods and findings of the Minneapolis Domestic Violence Police Experiment and five replication studies that attempted to test the deterrent effect on domestic violence of arrests and other police responses.

Methods

The methods of these studies are described in the summary of *"Does Arrest Deter Domestic Violence?"* by Janell D. Schmidt and Lawrence W. Sherman, which appears elsewhere in this publication.

---

[13] From *New England Law Review*, 28 (Summer 1994), 929.

Findings

The major research findings of the Minneapolis Domestic Violence Police Experiment and the replication studies are included in the above-referenced summary of *"Does Arrest Deter Domestic Violence?"*

Conclusions

There were fundamental design flaws in the studies, which included:

- Ignoring the fact that domestic violence, unchecked, usually escalates in frequency and severity.
- Failing to take into account the impact of postarrest decisions by prosecutors and courts.

Other design flaws included (in one or more studies):

- Instructing the police to discourage future police contacts by the victim.
- Including self-defense cases that have lesser deterrent possibilities.
- Assigning bad risks to the arrest category.
- Providing advance notice to responding officers about the response to be made.
- Failing to screen offenders for prior police contact.
- Failing to take into account victims' responses to offender arrests or the effect of the violence on others (e.g., children).
- Failing to randomly assign separated parties.

The policy value of the studies is limited since they:

- Were limited to misdemeanors.
- Did not address the effect of nonarrest.
- Isolated the initial police response from other possible responses to domestic abuse and studied only one of potentially dozens of issues that could have been studied.
- Ignored nondeterrence benefits of arrest, including immediate safety for the victim, access to services, and conveying a message that domestic violence is a crime.

Other conclusions include:

- While mandatory arrest may have no greater deterrent effect than other police responses, it is unclear as to whether or not it has a lesser deterrent effect.
- In the short term, mandatory arrest results in lower rates of recidivism than nonarrest police responses. It is likely, therefore, that later escalation is motivated by something other than anger or retaliation for arrest.
- Mandatory arrests are followed by a reduction of subsequent violence against victims of employed abusers and against white victims and Hispanic victims, and a slight increase in subsequent violence against black victims.
- Arrest without more follow-through by the criminal justice system may be too weak a sanction to deter many batterers.
- In addition to considering the deterrent effects of arrest, it is important to consider its effects on victims, children, and society.

Implications for Law Enforcement

With probable cause, police should:

- Arrest all abusers not acting in self-defense.
- Issue an arrest warrant even if the offender is absent.

A final implication: The length of time an arrested abuser is held should be no shorter than that of other offenders.

Selected Conclusions Drawn From

Mandatory Arrest of Batterers: A Reply to Its Critics

by Evan Stark[14]

Purpose of Research

To review and critique the assumptions, methods, and findings of the literature concluding that mandatory arrest policies are ineffective, including the Minneapolis police experiment and the five studies designed to replicate it, which attempted to test the deterrent effect on domestic violence of arrests and other police responses.

Methods

The methods of these studies are described in the summary of *"Does Arrest Deter Domestic Violence?"* by Janell D. Schmidt and Lawrence W. Sherman, elsewhere in this publication.

Findings

The major research findings of the Minneapolis Domestic Violence Police Experiment and the replication studies are described in the above-referenced summary of *"Does Arrest Deter Domestic Violence?"*

Conclusions

The author offers several conclusions regarding "proarrest" or mandatory arrest strategies:

- Proarrest strategy should be thought of as a "package of goods" that may include everything from a mere warning, handcuffing, or an arrest warrant through a weekend in jail, mandated treatment, a stalker's law, community intervention programs, the provision of court-based advocates, and real prison time.

- In addition to repeated physical abuse, woman battering typically includes a range of coercive strategies designed to dominate a partner. Many offenders respond to sanctions against physical abuse by isolating, intimidating, and controlling their partners. Therefore, mandatory arrest policies are best assessed by their overall effect on the victim's subordination rather than by the incidence of violence alone.

- There are reasons beyond deterrence for mandatory arrest policy. These include:

  — Providing a standard against which to judge variation in police response.

  — Providing immediate protection from current violence and giving victims time to consider their options.

  — Reducing the overall incidence of domestic violence both directly (because arrest might deter recidivism), and by sending a clear message that battering is unacceptable.

  — Acknowledging a special social interest in redressing the legacy of discriminatory treatment of women by law enforcement.

  — Serving a "redistributive" function by acknowledging that police service is a resource previously not available to women on an egalitarian basis.

  — Providing victims access to services and protection that would not be available outside the criminal justice system.

---

[14] From *Do Arrests and Restraining Orders Work?*, edited by Eve S. Buzawa and Carl G. Buzawa, Sage Publications, 1996.

Selected Findings and Implications Drawn From

Determining Police Response to Domestic Violence Victims

by Eve S. Buzawa and Thomas Austin[15]

Purpose of Research

To determine when and if victim preferences affect the decision to arrest domestic violence offenders and to determine victim satisfaction with police response.

Methods

The research was conducted in four precincts within the Detroit Police Department. Officers were instructed to complete Supplemental Arrest Reports in domestic assault cases to provide background information on the victim and offender, characteristics of the incident, seriousness of injury to the victim, the victim's preferred response, and the actual police response. The researchers analyzed 165 reports. In addition, 110 victims were randomly selected for in-person interviews.

Findings

An analysis of the Supplemental Arrest Reports found:

- The presence of bystanders or children during the abuse dramatically increased the chances that an arrest would be made.

- The presence of weapons affected how the officer handled the incident. The use of guns and sharp objects more often resulted in an arrest than the use of blunt objects or bodily weapons.

- When an injury resulted, officers were more likely to make an arrest.

- Arrests were more than twice as likely when the offender and victim shared the same residence. There was not, however, a statistically significant difference in arrest rates for married versus unmarried couples.

- About one-third of the victims told the officer they wanted prosecution; among those who expressed such a desire, arrests were made in 44 percent of the cases. When the victim did not want an arrest, an arrest was made in only 21 percent of the cases.

Interviews with the victims found:

- The large majority of victims (85 percent) were satisfied with the police response. They were especially satisfied when the police complied with their preferences regarding arresting (or not arresting) the offender.

- Most women victims were satisfied with the police response but not one male victim was.

Implications for Law Enforcement

With regard to victim preferences, it is recommended that police officers:

- Weigh more heavily the desires of victims about arresting (or not arresting) the offender. As a way to accomplish this, police reports could include victim preferences and if the officer disagreed with the victim preferences, he or she should state why.

- Increase their understanding of the dynamics of domestic violence cases through training; this is critical as this is correlated with officers taking victims' preferences seriously.

---

[15] From *American Behavioral Scientist*, 36 (5) (May 1993), 610–623.

Prosecution and Defense

Selected Findings and Implications Drawn From

Prosecution Response to Domestic Violence: Results of a Survey of Large Jurisdictions

by Donald J. Rebovich[16]

Purpose of Research

To assess the state of formal and informal domestic violence programs within local prosecutors' offices, identify needs of local prosecutors, explain common obstacles to successful prosecution of domestic violence, and recommend ways to improve the effectiveness of domestic violence prosecution.

Methods

Data were gathered from a national mail survey of 200 local prosecutors' offices, comprising all prosecutors' offices in jurisdictions with populations of more than 250,000. The response rate was 68 percent.

Findings

Data from the survey were grouped according to the following categories:

Case Management:

- Most prosecutors' offices handled both felony and misdemeanor domestic violence cases.
- The level of available resources affected the manner in which domestic violence cases were handled in most prosecutors' offices.

Case screening and charging:

- In more than three-quarters of the jurisdictions, domestic violence cases typically came into the prosecutor's office through the police rather than the victim.
- Most prosecutors' offices experienced screening and charging decisionmaking problems unique to domestic violence cases. Slightly more than half also used criteria unique to domestic violence cases in screening and charging these cases. Most proceeded with prosecution despite the noncooperation of the victim.
- Approximately two-thirds had formal office protocols for processing domestic violence cases, but fewer than a third had separate protocols for misdemeanors and felonies.
- Most large prosecutors' offices were in jurisdictions where proarrest policies have been adopted by local police departments. While proarrest policies affected the volume of domestic violence cases in these offices, they resulted in modified decisionmaking in fewer than a fifth of the offices and affected the plea negotiation process in even fewer.
- Two-thirds of the prosecutors' offices had no-drop policies, although there was usually some flexibility in these policies.

---

[16] From *Do Arrests and Restraining Orders Work?*, edited by Eve S. Buzawa and Carl G. Buzawa, Sage Publications, 1996. The study was funded under National Institute of Justice grant #93–IJ–CX–0039.

- The degree to which victim willingness to cooperate affected prosecutorial decisions varied according to size of the jurisdiction. In jurisdictions with populations of more than 500,000, only 8 percent of the respondents felt that victim cooperation affected their decision to prosecute to a high degree, whereas a third of those in jurisdictions between 250,000 and 500,000 felt that it affected the decision to a significant degree.

Pretrial release policies:

- Three-quarters of prosecutors recommended bail amounts comparable to those for other offenses. Almost all requested that certain conditions be set on the abuser's release.

- Slightly more than two-thirds of prosecutors in jurisdictions between 250,000 and 500,000 notified the victim of the defendant's release, while only half in jurisdictions with more than 500,000 did so.

- While most prosecutors relied on protective orders at least to a medium degree, only three-quarters found them effective, and two-thirds rated their effectiveness as only average.

- The presence of a child had a medium or high impact on how the prosecutor proceeded in nearly three-quarters of the jurisdictions.

Postcharge diversion:

- Half the prosecutors' offices used postcharge diversion and half did not. Where such programs existed, nearly two-thirds were pretrial and the rest were postplea. Generally, offenders who successfully completed the program were not prosecuted.

Trials:

- All jurisdictions in the study encountered victims who preferred not to be involved or come to court. Most also experienced victims who testified only upon subpoena, victim nonappearance upon subpoena, and active undermining of the prosecution by victims. A third of jurisdictions had uncooperative victims in slightly more than half of their cases.

- The most common method used to overcome problems connected with uncooperative domestic violence victims was the subpoena, used by most of the jurisdictions. A close second was the use of photographs of injuries to the victim. Other much less frequently used methods included evidence of "excited utterances" at the crime scene, family/neighbor testimony, 911 audiotapes, sworn statements, victim advocate testimony, and videotapes of initial victim interviews.

Sentencing options:

- About two-thirds of prosecutors believed sentences for domestic violence offenders in their jurisdictions were moderate and most of the rest believed they were lenient.

Victim support programs:

- Most prosecutors' offices employed some formal procedures to encourage victim participation in the prosecution process.

- The most common services were referral to social service agencies and court accompaniment of the victim. Others included court preparation, victim education about criminal/civil remedies, and supportive counseling.

Implications for Prosecutors

As growing numbers of police departments adopt proarrest policies for domestic violence offenses, prosecutors' offices are being faced with increasing numbers of domestic violence cases.

The study provides benchmarks against which prosecutors may compare their domestic violence policies and practices with those of their colleagues in other jurisdictions and learn of their colleagues' views on a number of issues.

It also raises—but does not generally provide definitive answers to—a number of important questions for prosecutors' offices. Among them:

- What, if any, aspects of domestic violence cases warrant unique screening criteria?
- What alternatives might be pursued when victims are noncooperative?
  - Subpoenas.
  - Photographs of injuries to the victim.
  - Evidence of "excited utterances" at the crime scene.
  - Family or neighbor testimony.
  - Use of 911 audiotapes.
  - Sworn statements.
  - Victim advocate testimony.
  - Videotapes of initial victim interviews.
- Is a "no drop" policy appropriate? If so, are there any exceptions?
- Should bail amounts be different for domestic violence cases than for other cases? What about other conditions of pretrial release?
- Should victims be notified of defendants' pretrial release?
- When should protective orders be recommended? What is the appropriate extent of followup to ensure enforcement of protective orders?
- How should the presence of a child affect the decision whether or not to prosecute?
- Should postcharge diversion be an option? If so, should it be used pretrial or postplea? If a defendant successfully completes the diversion program, should the charges be dropped? Should lesser charges be pursued?
- What formal procedures should be employed to encourage victim participation in the prosecution process?
  - Referral to social service agencies.
  - Court accompaniment of the victim.
  - Court preparation of the victim.
  - Victim education about criminal/civil remedies.
  - Supportive counseling.
- What, if any, protocols should differ for misdemeanor domestic violence offenses and felony domestic violence offenses?
- What (additional) resources are needed to implement desirable domestic violence policies? What are the priorities?

Selected Findings and Implications Drawn From

The Indianapolis Domestic Violence Prosecution Experiment

by David A. Ford and Mary Jean Regoli[17]

Purpose of Research

To examine the effectiveness of alternative prosecutorial policies in reducing renewed violence by misdemeanor battery defendants against their partners.

Methods

The research consisted of two randomized experiments. One involved on-scene arrests (OSAs) of 198 suspects by police responding to violent domestic disturbances, and the other involved 480 suspects who were the subject of victim complaints (VCs) filed in person with the prosecutor's office. OSA cases could not be dropped by the victims, and were randomly assigned to one of three prosecutorial policy tracks: (1) pretrial diversion involving rehabilitative counseling; (2) adjudicated guilt with counseling as a condition of probation; and (3) other sentencing such as fines, probation, and jail time. VC cases had a fourth randomized policy track whereby victims were allowed to drop charges; in addition, the defendants in VC cases were randomly assigned to be brought to court through either a warrant or a summons. Accordingly, there were eight combinations for VC cases compared to three for OSA cases.

Six months after court settlement, victims and accused offenders were interviewed and official records examined to determine whether any of the alternative criminal justice policies had influenced the prevalence, severity, and frequency of subsequent violence.

Findings

The study revealed:

- Domestic violence victims were considerably more likely to have been battered in the 6 months before their cases were brought to the prosecutor than in the 6 months following settlement (more than 70 percent before vs. fewer than 40 percent after).

- Battering did not necessarily stop between the time accused batterers were arrested or summoned to court and the time their cases were settled. Approximately 20 percent of defendants arrested on the scene or as a result of warrants issued in response to formal victim complaints rebattered their victims before case settlement, as did 27 percent of defendants summoned to court following formal victim complaints.

- Regardless of particular prosecutorial policies pursued and methods of bringing defendants to court, there was considerable rebattering in the 6 months following case settlement. However, in victim-initiated cases, the manner whereby defendants were brought to court and the specific prosecutorial policies followed significantly affected the extent of rebattering:

    — In cases initiated by warrantless on-scene arrests, nearly 40 percent of defendants rebattered their partners within 6 months of settlement. None of the three prosecutorial policies (pretrial diversion to rehabilitative counseling,

---

[17] From a Final Report submitted to the National Institute of Justice, October 1993, NCJ 157870. Research was conducted under NIJ grant #86–IJ–CX–0012 by David A. Ford, Department of Sociology, Indiana University at Indianapolis and University Research Associates, and by Mary Jean Regoli, Indiana University at Bloomington.

adjudicated guilt with counseling as a condition of probation, or traditional sentencing) had a unique preventative impact on the prevalence, severity, or frequency of rebattering.

— In cases initiated by formal victim complaints, 29 percent of defendants battered their partners again within 6 months of settlement. However, arresting defendants by warrant and allowing victims to drop charges resulted in a rebattering rate (13 percent) less than half that of each of the other seven prosecution possibilities. Summoning defendants to court and pursuing noncounseling sentencing alternatives resulted in the highest rebattering rate (44 percent).

— Moreover, while fewer than 20 percent of all subjects of victim complaints engaged in severe followup violence within 6 months of settlement, 36 percent of those summoned to court and prosecuted on noncounseling sentencing tracks did so.

- When victims were allowed to drop complaints they had filed (whether resulting in warrant or summons), those who elected to go forth with the prosecution were significantly less likely to be rebattered than those who did not. Those who dropped charges after the batterer was summoned to court were in greatest jeopardy of renewed violence.

- Regardless of the prosecutorial track pursued, desired court outcomes resulted more frequently when cases were initiated by victim complaints (67 percent of the cases) than when they were initiated by on-scene arrests (58 percent).

- The lowest rates of followup violence were associated with findings of "not guilty." Other court outcomes did not significantly affect the prevalence of followup violence.

- Regardless of whether cases were initiated by on-scene arrests or by victim complaints and regardless of the prosecutorial track taken, most victims reported feeling more secure and in control 6 months after their cases were settled than they did before prosecutorial action was taken.

Implications for Prosecutors

The following practical implications were drawn:

- Prosecutors can help victims minimize the chance of violence by affirming the legitimacy of their criminal complaints and by respecting their decisions about what is best under their unique circumstances, even if contrary to the prosecutor's administrative concerns.

- Since victims are frequently battered between the time a defendant is arrested or a complaint is filed and the time the case is settled, prosecutors can support and hopefully protect victims by attending to their interests throughout the prosecution process, for example, by monitoring warrants to see they are served in a timely manner; by requesting protection orders and seeing that they are aggressively enforced; by watching for evidence of obstruction of justice in defense attorneys' contacts with victims; and by making every effort to account for a victim's safety.

- Prosecutors should review their own prosecution policies in terms of their effectiveness in reducing followup violence.*

- Prosecutors who allow victims to drop their complaints should explain to them that dropping the charges might entail increased risk of violence.*

---

* These implications are not explicit in the report but appear to follow from the findings and conclusions.

- Prosecutors who respond to victim complaints by issuing summonses to alleged batterers should consider whether warrants might result in less rebattering, especially if victims are allowed to drop charges or cases are generally put on a traditional sentencing track.*

- Before diverting accused batterers to counseling programs or recommending probation with counseling, prosecutors should be informed about the long-range success rates of available counseling programs since, at least in the short term, counseling alternatives are no more effective than traditional sentences in reducing followup battering.*

Implications for Judges

In sentencing batterers, judges should take into account that, at least in the short term, probation with counseling may be no more effective in reducing followup violence than traditional sentences. Judges should seek evidence that counseling programs available in their jurisdictions are effective in preventing violence or, if honoring a victim's request for mandated counseling, that the counseling will not result in further harm.*

Selected Findings and Implications Drawn From

Validity of "Battered Woman Syndrome" in Criminal Cases Involving Battered Women

by Malcolm Gordon[18]

Purpose of Research

To compile information about "medical and psychological testimony on the validity of battered women's syndrome as a condition" (as required in the 1994 Violence Against Women Act).

Method

The study consisted of a review of literature concerning scientific and clinical knowledge about battering and its effects, the implications of this scientific knowledge for criminal cases involving battered women, and the role of expert testimony in criminal cases involving battered women.

Findings

The term "battered woman syndrome" wrongly implies that all battered women respond similarly to being battered and that the common response includes inability to defend themselves, posttraumatic stress distress, and a pathological or maladjusted mental state.

In fact, battered women may experience a wide range of traumatic psychological reactions to being battered, which may affect:

- Continued involvement in an abusive relationship.

- Use of physical aggression toward the abuser.

- Future appraisal of the threat of violence.

---

* These implications are not explicit in the report but appear to follow from the findings and conclusions.

[18] From an edited version of a review paper prepared by Mary Ann Dutton, *"The Validity and Use of Evidence Concerning Battering and Its Effects in Criminal Trials: A Report to Congress Under the Violence Against Women Act,"* Research Report, Washington, D.C.: U.S. Department of Justice, National Institute of Justice and the U.S. Department of Health and Human Services, National Institute of Mental Health, May 1996, NCJ 160972.

- Involvement in other criminal activity.
- Refusal or reluctance to cooperate in prosecuting the abuser because of fear of retaliation.

Battered women also experience negative psychological consequences of domestic violence, which may include:

- Amnesia.
- Re-experiencing the trauma (e.g., flashbacks).
- Absence of emotional reactions.
- Hostile or angry reactions.
- Depression.

Additional findings included that:

- Battered women may continue their involvement in abusive relationships because of:
  — Economic factors.
  — Fear that violence will escalate if there is an attempt to leave.
  — Fear that the abuser might retaliate by legally or illegally taking the children.
  — Emotional attachment to the abuser.
- It is a myth that battered women are passive about their victimization; many do fight back either physically or verbally, or engage in other active efforts to resist, avoid, escape, and stop the violence against them.
- A battered woman's appraisal of the threat implicit in a batterer's behavior is based on the pattern of the batterer's prior violence and abuse, the actual threat, the timing of the threat, and the victim's state of mind at the time of the threat.
- There is no one pattern that characterizes all batterers' behavior. Several recognized patterns include:
  — A "cycle of violence" with a series of stages with differing levels of positive and negative emotional engagement, coercion, and physical aggression. These stages may include tension-building, acute-battering, and contrite-loving phases.
  — A long period of time between acute battering episodes.
  — "Separation abuse" where the batterer threatens violence or retaliates violently if the victim separates from the batterer either physically or by making herself unavailable (e.g., becoming involved in a new relationship or beginning divorce proceedings).
- Battered women may fail to cooperate with prosecution as a way to avoid retaliation by their abusers or as a way of avoiding painful and distressing emotions that cooperation would entail.
- Because battering and the effects of battering vary from case to case, there is no "battered woman defense" *per se*.
- Nevertheless, evidence and expert testimony about battering and its effects can assist the factfinder in putting battered women's actions in context in criminal proceedings involving:
  — Self-defense or insanity defense of a battered woman who has murdered or assaulted her batterer.
  — Charging or sentencing a battered woman who has murdered or assaulted her batterer.
  — Duress defense of a battered woman who has committed criminal or illegal conduct through the instigation or coercion of a perpetrator.
  — Prosecution of alleged perpetrators of domestic violence.

Such testimony can also dispel misconceptions about domestic violence that might be held by a judge or jury.

- Expert testimony about battering may be either general (providing information about the scientific and clinical knowledge about battering without relating the information to a specific individual) or specific (based on an evaluation of a specific individual).

Implications for Defense Attorneys

Expert testimony on domestic violence may be useful in supporting a plea of self-defense, an insanity defense, or a duress defense. It may also be used to support mitigating factors in charging and sentencing and to explain misconceptions about domestic violence to judges and juries.

Implications for Prosecutors

Expert testimony may be useful in supporting the prosecution of defendants accused of domestic violence by explaining the victim's recantation of previous statements, refusal or unwillingness to proceed, and other behavior that might otherwise be detrimental to the prosecution, and by explaining misconceptions about domestic violence to judges and juries.

Selected Findings and Implications Drawn From

Impact of Evidence Concerning Battering and Its Effects in Criminal Trials Involving Battered Women

by Mary Ann Dutton[19]

Purpose of Research

To assess the effects that evidence of battered woman syndrome may have in criminal trials.

Method

The findings were based on a 3-day focus group meeting attended by Federal, State, and tribal court judges, prosecutors, defense attorneys, expert witnesses, and advocates.

Findings

Results from the panel discussion included:

- Expert testimony concerning battering and its effects can help factfinders more effectively assess evidence in criminal cases involving battered women.

- Expert testimony concerning battering and its effects can also dispel common myths and misunderstandings concerning domestic violence, including stereotypes of both battered women and batterers, that may interfere with the factfinders' ability to assess the case.

- Despite precedent for referring to expert testimony in cases involving battered women as "battered woman syndrome" testimony, the term is both too ambiguous and too narrow to help factfinders understand the evidence or determine facts in issue. As with other victims of violence, there is no single set of effects that characterize all battered women, but rather a range of effects. References to "battered woman syndrome" should be replaced by references to "battering and its effects."

---

[19] From *The Validity and Use of Evidence Concerning Battering and Its Effects in Criminal Trials: A Report to Congress under the Violence Against Women Act*, Research Report, Washington, D.C.: U.S. Department of Justice, National Institute of Justice and U.S. Department of Health and Human Services, National Institute of Mental Health, May 1996, NCJ 160972.

- There is a continuing need to educate judges, prosecutors, and defense attorneys about effectively incorporating into criminal trials available expertise concerning battering and its effects.

- There is an increased need for resources for expert witnesses to consult with attorneys and testify in criminal cases.

- Testimony from "nonprofessionals" experienced in working with battered women (e.g., shelter workers, police officers, trauma technicians, hotline workers) should be considered admissible. While such individuals are not qualified to conduct psychological testing, they should be allowed to testify about their observations and knowledge of battered women's experiences generally and their observations of particular battered women based on their expertise.

- The development of domestic violence coordinating councils has been associated with the introduction of evidence concerning battering and its effects into the courtroom. Often headed by the court, these councils typically include representatives from the prosecutor's office, law enforcement, batterer treatment programs, battered women's shelters, schools, hospitals, law clinics, child welfare agencies, and other government agencies and organizations.

Implications for Judges

Judges who handle cases involving domestic violence would benefit from the following:

- A basic understanding of battering and its effects to determine the relevancy of expert witness testimony to the issues at hand and to rule on issues such as jury instructions and the scope of expert testimony to be allowed before the triers of fact.

- A general understanding of various scientific methods used in domestic violence research (e.g., experimental design, correlational, factor analysis, descriptive, or qualitative) to determine the validity of scientific evidence about battering and its effects.

- Judicial education programs to increase their substantive knowledge about domestic violence and the methods of scientific inquiry related to it. The State Justice Institute, the National Judicial College, the National Council of Juvenile and Family Court Judges, and the American Bar Association Judicial Administration Division are among groups active in promoting and sponsoring judicial education about domestic violence.

Implications for Defense Attorneys

Defense attorneys can learn more about battering by attending continuing legal education programs on the topic and by consulting with expert witnesses. Consultants may be shelter workers, battered woman advocates, counselors, psychologists, psychiatrists, or social workers. Defense attorneys with knowledge about battering and the effects it has on victims would be able to recognize the following:

- Relevant evidence on the subject when defending battered women charged with crimes.

- Relevant expert testimony about battering not only in cases where self-defense can be asserted but also in other cases (e.g., where the woman commits a crime under the coercion of her batterer).

- Evidence about battering relevant to evaluation of clemency petitions.

- Potential ramifications of prosecutorial use of expert testimony regarding battering and its effects when defending alleged batterers.

Implications for Prosecutors

Prosecutors also can learn more about battering by attending continuing legal education programs on the topic and by consultation with expert witnesses. Consultants may be shelter workers, battered woman advocates, counselors, psychologists, psychiatrists, or social workers. Education on battering and its effects is critical for prosecutors to help them:

- Recognize and introduce relevant evidence on the subject when prosecuting alleged batterers.

- Use expert testimony in cases against the batterer to explain why the battered woman has previously recanted testimony, is unwilling to cooperate with the prosecution, or has engaged in behavior that the factfinder may find puzzling.

- Recognize the importance of paying considerable attention to battering issues at the charging stage, whether or not a grand jury is involved.

- Be aware of the potential ramifications of the defense use of expert testimony regarding battering and its effects.

Selected Findings and Implications Drawn From

Trend Analysis: Expert Testimony on Battering and its Effects in Criminal Cases

by Janet Parrish[20]

Purpose of Research

To capture current trends in court decisions and statutes regarding the use of expert testimony on battering and its effects and to highlight various ways expert testimony can ensure that relevant evidence about battering is introduced at the trials of battered women or their alleged batterers.

Research Methods

The study analyzed 238 State and 31 Federal court decisions (mostly appellate) in cases where women defendants introduced—or tried to introduce—expert witnesses at their trials, and 12 State statutes relating to the use of expert testimony on battering and its effects in criminal cases.

Research Findings

An analysis of the court decisions revealed:

- There is no "battered woman's defense" *per se*; expert testimony on battering and its effects can only be used to support—not to supplant—a battered woman's use of traditional self-defense or duress claims.

- Since the mid-1980s, courts have increasingly recognized the relevance of expert testimony about battering and its effects. Such testimony has been admitted to at least some degree in the District of Columbia and each of the 50 States. Of the 19 Federal courts that have considered the issue, all but 3 have admitted the testimony in at least some cases.

- Expert testimony on battering and its effects has been most readily accepted by State courts in cases involving traditional self-defense situations.

---

[20] From *The Validity and Use of Evidence Concerning Battering and its Effects in Criminal Trials: A Report to Congress under the Violence Against Women Act*, Research Report, Washington, D.C.: U.S. Department of Justice, National Institute of Justice and U.S. Department of Health and Human Services, National Institute of Mental Health, May 1996, NCJ 160972.

- A substantial number of States have also admitted expert testimony on battering and its effects in nontraditional self-defense situations (e.g., when a battered woman kills her batterer while he is sleeping or hires a third party to kill him).

- Some State and Federal courts have admitted expert testimony on battering and its effects in non-self-defense cases (e.g., where duress is asserted as a defense or where a battered woman has been charged with a crime against a third party).

- Most States have admitted expert testimony on battering and its effects to prove the defendant is a battered woman. However, in many of these States, the testimony must be "generic," that is, used to explain battering and its effects generally without reference to the specific defendant.

- Most States have found expert testimony relevant to supporting a self-defense claim (assessing the reasonableness of the defendant's belief she was in danger of imminent harm and/or of her actions in defense of herself or others) and to assessing the woman's state of mind at the time of the charged crime.

- More States have precluded expert opinions on whether the defendant acted reasonably or in self-defense than have allowed such opinions.

- Most States consider expert testimony on battering and its effects relevant to explaining a battered woman's conduct, including why she did not leave the battering relationship or committed certain acts.

- Some States have found expert testimony to be admissible to:
    — Prove a defendant's diminished capacity, mental defect, or lack of intent.
    — Bolster the defendant's credibility.
    — Show the existence of mitigating factors at the sentencing phase of the trial.

- Most States that have considered whether expert testimony on battering and its effects subjects the defendant to an adverse psychological examination have concluded that it does.

- The majority of courts that have considered whether failure to offer expert testimony on battering and its effects constitutes ineffective assistance of counsel have found that it does not. Moreover, the few States that have considered whether indigent battered women must be afforded State funds to hire expert witnesses have found that the funds can be denied (although one such decision was reversed in Federal court).

- Appeals courts affirmed nearly two-thirds of the State convictions appealed by women who had introduced or tried to introduce expert testimony about battering and its effects at their trials. In nearly three-quarters of the cases where convictions were affirmed, expert testimony had been admitted or found admissible. Erroneous exclusion of, limitation of, or failure of counsel to present expert testimony accounted for less than half of the convictions that were reversed.

- Expert testimony on battering and its effects has been admitted in some States when offered by the prosecution (e.g., to explain a battered woman complainant's prior inconsistent statements).

Implications for Defense Attorneys*

Defense attorneys should be aware of the statutes and case law in their jurisdictions and, if applicable, in the Federal statutes and case law, regarding:

- General admissibility of expert testimony.
- General exclusion of expert testimony.

---

* These implications are not explicit in the report but appear to follow from the findings.

- Specific types of cases in which expert testimony is admissible or excluded, including "traditional" and "nontraditional" self-defense cases and non-self-defense cases.

- The showing necessary for introduction of expert testimony, including whether or not there must be a self-defense claim; evidence that battering (or the "battered woman's syndrome") is accepted in the scientific community; certain qualifications of the expert; and a showing that the defendant is, in fact, battered.

- Ineffective counsel issues (outcome of appeals asserting ineffective counsel on grounds of failure to offer expert testimony on battering and its effects).

- Issues relating to State funding for expert testimony (decisions relating to whether States must provide funding for expert testimony).

- The scope and relevance of expert testimony (admissibility of expert testimony to prove the defendant is a battered woman and/or to explain battering and its effects generally; admissibility of expert opinion as to whether the defendant herself is a battered woman).

Implications for Prosecutors*

Prosecutors should be aware of the statutes and case law in their jurisdictions and, if applicable, Federal statutes and case law, as they relate to:

- Prosecution of battered women on charges related to the murder or injury of their batterers or for other crimes where the defense is duress. (See specifics under "Implications for Defense Attorneys," above.)

- Prosecution of alleged batterers and admissibility of expert testimony on battering and its effects to explain certain behaviors of battered women, that is, staying with the batterer, prior inconsistent statements, and previous failure to pursue charges.

---

* These implications are not explicit in the report but appear to follow from the findings.

Selected Findings and Implications Drawn From

Prosecuting Domestic Violence Cases With Reluctant Victims: Assessing Two Novel Approaches in Milwaukee

by Robert C. Davis, Barbara E. Smith, and Laura Nickles[21]

Purpose of Research

To assess the impact of two domestic violence projects implemented in Milwaukee, Wisconsin. The first examined the effectiveness of a specialized domestic violence court designed to speed up case processing time. The second examined the effect of a subsequent change in the district attorney's screening policy that admitted more cases into the special court.

Methods

Data were collected from each of three periods: prior to September 1994 (the start of the special domestic violence court), between September 1994 and January 1995 (the period after the special court began and before the change in the district attorney's charging policy), and after January 1995 (after the change in the district attorney's charging policy). Data were collected from prosecutors' files, police reports of new arrests for offenders, and via interviews with victims.

Findings

After the creation of the specialized court:

- Processing time was halved.
- Convictions were up by 25 percent.
- Pretrial crime declined.
- The prevalence of new felony arrests showed a slight but statistically nonsignificant reduction.

After introduction of a new liberalized district attorney charging policy:

- Case backlog increased greatly.
- Cases filed with the court contained a higher proportion of victims who did not want their cases prosecuted.
- Time to case disposition doubled.
- Convictions declined.
- Pretrial crime increased.
- Victim satisfaction with case outcomes and with the prosecutor's handling of the case declined.

The researchers concluded as follows:

- The study produced evidence that the theory on which the domestic violence court was based was sound. Reducing processing time produced concomitant changes in convictions and opportunities for pretrial crime.

- What was accomplished in the Milwaukee domestic violence court was highly significant. It is one of the few documented successful attempts to address the problem of low convictions in domestic violence cases. It was done without coercion of victims (as is the case in jurisdictions that institute no-drop policies) and without additional resources.

- The district attorney's policy to prosecute a larger proportion of domestic violence arrests had several effects, none of them positive, which may have been due in part to insufficient allocation of resources. One

---

[21] From a Final Report to the National Institute of Justice by the American Bar Association's Criminal Justice Section; funded by NIJ grant #95–IJ–CX–0105, April 1997, NCJ 169111.

effect of the new policy was to bring into the court system a larger proportion of cases with victims who were not interested in seeing the defendant prosecuted. Victim satisfaction with prosecutors and with court outcomes declined after the new screening policy. As the special court became overwhelmed with cases, case processing time increased back to the level that had existed prior to the start of the specialized court.

Implications for Criminal Court Officials

The researchers drew the following implications:

- Shortening court processing time in domestic violence cases is a good idea. It has been shown to decrease pretrial crime and increase conviction rates.

- Introducing domestic violence cases with reluctant victims into the criminal justice system should be carefully considered. Potential benefits may result, but negative results were noted in the Milwaukee study. These types of cases were found to increase case processing time, increase pretrial crime, decrease convictions, and decrease satisfaction with prosecutor handling and court outcome.

- Should the decision be made to introduce cases with reluctant victims, sufficient resources should be allocated to adequately prosecute and adjudicate the cases. In Milwaukee, there was no increase in victim/witness, prosecutorial, or judicial staff to handle twice the number of cases the district attorney entered into the court system.

- In deciding whether or not to prosecute, the victim's voice should be carefully considered. It may be justified to go counter to victims' wishes not to prosecute in select cases where there is a clear indication (e.g., by virtue of prior history and dangerousness of the defendant) that harm will come to victims if defendants are not prosecuted. However, to completely ignore victims' wishes is likely to produce a caseload with many unwinnable cases and disgruntled victims.

Court-Ordered Treatment

Selected Findings and Implications Drawn From

The Impact of Court-Ordered Treatment for Domestic Violence Offenders

by Adele Harrell[22]

Purpose of Research

To evaluate the impact of court-ordered treatment for domestic violence abusers.

Methods

Research was based on quasi-experimental design with a total sample of 193 "male against female" misdemeanor domestic abuse offenders in five district courts in Baltimore County, Maryland, between September 1988 and October 1989. Rotating judges with different treatment/nontreatment preferences ordered the abusers to treatment in one of three available treatment programs. The study compared 81 treated offenders with 112 offenders not ordered to treatment. The cessation of subsequent severe violence, physical aggression, threats and the frequency of physical aggression, and psychological abuse were measured by interviews with victims and abusers 1 month after case disposition and again 4 to 6 months later.

Findings[23]

Study comparisons of treated and nontreated offenders indicated:

- Treatment did not reduce the prevalence or frequency of violence:

  — Treated and nontreated abusers were not significantly different in terms of ceasing severe violence or threats of violence. Moreover, those *not* treated were significantly *less likely* than those treated to continue engaging in physical aggression.

  — While psychological abuse occurred significantly less frequently for treated abusers, treated and nontreated abusers were not significantly different in terms of the frequency of physical aggression and threats of violence.

- Offender characteristics that did not reduce frequency of violence were offender age, employment status, history of domestic violence, past criminal history, children living with the victim, and violent victimization of the offender as a child. Moreover, neither arresting the offender nor deferring prosecution had a significant effect on the frequency of posttreatment violence.

---

[22] From a Paper presented at the 44th Annual Meeting of The American Society of Criminology, New Orleans, Louisiana, November 4–7, 1992. The research was supported by the State Justice Institute, grant #90–12L–E–089.

[23] Researcher's caution: The treatment programs studied may have been too short or insufficiently intense, or may have used ineffective strategies; they may have been inadequately implemented; or their failure to sanction for noncompliance may have reduced the treatment impact. The author recommends that the study be replicated.

The following variables affected the impact of treatment:

- Among cases with a history of severe violence, treated offenders who were married to or living with the victim were significantly more likely to cease severe violence.

- Among cases with a history of physical aggression, treated offenders who were involved with drugs or alcohol use of whose victims had children living with them were significantly more likely to cease physical aggression.

- Treated offenders with a past criminal record were significantly more likely than other offenders to be involved in a subsequent incident.

Implications for Judges and Court Practitioners

Courts need to closely examine:

- Practices such as long delays in hearing cases and in starting treatment when ordering offenders to treatment.

- Monitoring of compliance with treatment orders and the provision of sanctions for noncompliance.

- Victims' protection needs while offenders are in treatment.

- Alternative sanctions to be used in combination with or in place of treatment that will protect the interests of victims of domestic violence.

Selected Findings and Implications Drawn From

The Role of Drug and Alcohol Abuse in Domestic Violence and Its Treatment: Dade County's Domestic Violence Court Experiment

by John S. Goldkamp, with Doris Weiland, Mark Collins and Michael White[24]

Purpose of Research

To obtain baseline data on domestic violence offenders and offenses, including data about the role of substance abuse in domestic violence and the dropout and rearrest rates of those ordered to treatment; and to compare the impact on treatment status and reinvolvement in the criminal and civil justice systems of two treatment approaches for domestic violence batterers: (1) the regular "dual" approach in which batterer treatment and alcohol/drug treatment are separate, with substance abuse treatment an "add-on" to batterer treatment and (2) a new "integrated" approach merging substance abuse and batterer treatment.

Methods

The two-phase project took place in the specialized treatment-oriented Dade County (Florida) Domestic Violence Court. The baseline study included a review of misdemeanor cases processed in the court for a 1-year period prior to the availability of integrated batterer/substance abuse treatment.

In the experiment, misdemeanor divertees and probationers ordered to treatment for both substance abuse and battering between early June 1994 and late February 1995 were randomly assigned to either the regular dual treatment process (n=140) or the new integrated

---

[24] From the Executive Summary of a Crime and Justice Research Institute study funded by the National Institute of Justice, grant #93–IJ–CX–0028, June 1994, NCJ 163411. The findings—particularly from the baseline study—were broader than those directly relevant to substance abuse that are described here.

treatment program (n=210). The progress of individuals in both groups was observed for 7 months to determine treatment status and to chart reinvolvement in the criminal and civil justice systems.

Findings

Among the findings in the baseline study of immediate relevance to the followup treatment experiment were the following:

- Roughly half of misdemeanor defendants in entering cases were involved in the abuse of alcohol and/or other drugs. However, fewer than half of the defendants so involved were processed into substance abuse treatment. Many of the cases with drug or alcohol involvement were dismissed or "no-actioned."

- Slightly more than half of the defendants were diverted or placed on probation. Nearly all divertees and probationers were assigned to domestic violence treatment; about two-fifths were also assigned to substance abuse evaluation and/or treatment.

- Large numbers of divertees and probationers assigned to treatment failed to appear at treatment programs.

- Higher rearrest rates were found among divertees and probationers who were not admitted to treatment. Rates of rearrest were lower for those who were admitted and "continued in process."

- Higher treatment dropout rates were found among those substance abuse-involved divertees and probationers who were assigned to batterer treatment and substance abuse treatment in separate programs than among those assigned to batterer programs only.

The treatment experiment yielded three statistically significant findings:

- The integrated treatment approach was far more successful than the dual process in getting divertees and probationers to begin treatment (43 percent of the dual program participants never showed up for treatment after intake compared to 13 percent of the integrated program participants).

- The integrated approach was more successful than the dual process at keeping participants in treatment (median of 160 days compared to 99).

- During the 7-month followup, participants in the integrated treatment program were rearrested for same-victim domestic violence offenses at less than half the rate of those assigned to dual programs (6 percent vs. 14 percent).

Implications for Judges*

The following implications were drawn:

- Since the fact and length of treatment favorably impact rearrest rates, judges should attempt to identify treatment programs that have demonstrated the ability to admit and keep in treatment domestic violence offenders with substance abuse problems, and should maintain contact with offenders to ensure they are attending treatment. (It is difficult to discern whether the treatment's effect on rearrest is because of the treatment itself or because the offender had more contacts with the court.)

- When the option is available, judges should consider ordering domestic violence offenders with substance abuse problems to integrated batterer/substance abuse treatment programs rather than to separate programs for batterer treatment and substance abuse treatment.

---

* These implications are not explicit in the report but appear to follow from the findings.

Other

Selected Findings and Implications Drawn From

Corporate Sector Response to Domestic Violence

by Nancy E. Isaac[25]

Purpose of Research

To explore what role the corporate sector is playing in responding to partner abuse as it impacts upon the health and safety of employees in the workplace.

Methods

The research findings were based on (1) interviews with corporate professionals in a variety of companies that examined their level of awareness and attitudes about partner violence and its potential effects on employees' work lives and (2) surveys with employee assistance professionals (EAPs) that examined how the corporate sector views the impact of partner violence on its employees.

Findings

The interview study found:

- Most executives and managers in the corporate sector have given little or no thought to the impact of partner abuse on the health and safety of their employees.

- Among larger companies, the EAP and security departments are the most aware of the potential impact of partner abuse on employees' work lives. There is little communication across departments within companies about this issue.

- Potential barriers to understanding and helping employees who are victims of partner abuse include lack of awareness, denial, embarrassment, privacy and confidentiality concerns, victim blaming, expectations of self-identification by abused women, fear of advocating for change, and concern that outreach to abused women may alienate male employees, damage the company image, or be too expensive.

The EAP survey found:

- A large majority of EAP providers have been faced with cases of partner abuse, including restraining order violations and stalking in the workplace.

- General policies on "workplace violence" exist in many companies but few specifically address domestic violence.

- There is increasing awareness among EAP staff that employees may bring domestic violence problems to the EAP.

- Among larger corporations, EAP staff are using a range of practices to assist employees impacted by abuse, including the use of a leave of absence, medical leave, and short-term disability.

- EAP staff expressed an interest in learning more about partner abuse and its potential impact on employees.

---

[25] From a Summary Report to National Institute of Justice under grant #94–IJ–CX–0050 to the Harvard School of Public Health, 1997, NCJ 166616.

- Interaction with the criminal justice sector with respect to domestic violence is limited. Only a handful of corporations have received training from police or other criminal justice officials. Further, three-quarters of EAP staff thought there was inadequate follow-through by the criminal justice system when a case of partner abuse was reported.

Implications for Interactions Between Companies and the Criminal Justice System

Companies should develop ties with the criminal justice sector. Suggestions included:

- Inviting local law enforcement officials to train key corporate staff and to provide an overview of local, State, and Federal statutes related to family violence.

- Developing ongoing contacts in criminal justice agencies and in particular in the domestic violence units of local law enforcement and prosecutor's offices.

Statistical Reports on Family Violence

Child Maltreatment 1995: Report From the States to the National Child Abuse and Neglect Data System, annual report, U.S. Department of Health and Human Services, 1997

(The) Crime of Stalking: How Big Is the Problem?, summary of a presentation by Patricia Tjaden, Center for Policy Research, National Institute of Justice "Research Preview," November 1996

Criminal Victimization in the United States, 1994: A National Crime Victimization Survey Report, Bureau of Justice Statistics, Tina Dorsey and Jayne Robinson, May 1997 (NCJ 162126)*

(The) Cycle of Violence, National Institute of Justice "Research in Brief," Cathy Spatz Widom, October 1992 (NCJ 136607)*

Domestic Violence and Sexual Violence Data Collection: A Report to Congress Under the Violence Against Women Act, Justice Research and Statistics Association, James Zepp, a joint publication of the National Institute of Justice and the Bureau of Justice Statistics, July 1996 (NCJ 161405)*

Domestic Violence, Stalking, and Antistalking Legislation: An Annual Report to Congress under the Violence Against Women Act, Mary Graham, ed., National Institute of Justice, April 1996 (NCJ 160943)*

Drugs, Alcohol, and Domestic Violence in Memphis, summary of a presentation by Daniel Brookoff, National Institute of Justice "Research Preview," October 1997

Elderly Crime Victims, Bureau of Justice Statistics "Selected Findings" from the National Crime Victimization Survey, March 1994 (NCJ 147186)*

Female Victims of Violent Crime, Bureau of Justice Statistics, December 1996 (NCJ 162602)*

Murder in Families, Bureau of Justice Statistics "Special Report," John M. Dawson and Patrick A. Langan, July 1994 (NCJ 143498)*

Partner Violence Among Young Adults, summary of a presentation by Terrie E. Moffitt, National Institute of Justice "Research Preview," April 1997

Sex Differences in Violent Victimization, 1994, Bureau of Justice Statistics "Special Report," Diane Craven, September 1997 (NCJ 164508)*

Spouse Murder Defendants in Large Urban Counties, Bureau of Justice Statistics "Executive Summary," Patrick A. Langan and John M. Dawson, September 1995 (NCJ 156831)*; full report, October 1995 (NCJ 153256)*

Stalking in America: Findings from the National Violence Against Women Survey, Patricia Tjaden and Nancy Thoennes, Center for Policy Research, July 1997 (NIJ grant #93–IJ–CX–0012)

Third National Incidence Study of Child Abuse and Neglect, U.S. Department of Health and Human Services, 1996

Violence Against Women: Estimates from the Redesigned Survey, Bureau of Justice Statistics "Special Report" on the National Crime Victimization Survey, Ronet Bachman and Linda E. Saltzman, August 1995 (NCJ 154348)*

Violence Against Women: A National Crime Victimization Survey Report, Bureau of Justice Statistics, Ronet Bachman, January 1994 (NCJ 145325)*

Violence Between Intimates, Bureau of Justice Statistics, November 1994 (NCJ 149259)*

Violence Between Intimates: 1992-1995, Bureau of Justice Statistics, forthcoming (NCJ 167237)*

*NCJ documents can be obtained from the National Criminal Justice Reference Service. Most are free of charge. E-mail at "askncjrs" or call 800–851–3420.

For more information on the National Institute of Justice, please contact:

National Criminal Justice Reference Service
Box 6000
Rockville, MD 20849–6000
800–851–3420
e-mail: askncjrs@ncjrs.org

To access the World Wide Web site, go to
http://www.ncjrs.org

If you have any questions, call or e-mail NCJRS.

About the National Institute of Justice

The National Institute of Justice (NIJ), a component of the Office of Justice Programs, is the research agency of the U.S. Department of Justice. Created by the Omnibus Crime Control and Safe Streets Act of 1968, as amended, NIJ is authorized to support research, evaluation, and demonstration programs, development of technology, and both national and international information dissemination. Specific mandates of the Act direct NIJ to:

- Sponsor special projects, and research and development programs, that will improve and strengthen the criminal justice system and reduce or prevent crime.
- Conduct national demonstration projects that employ innovative or promising approaches for improving criminal justice.
- Develop new technologies to fight crime and improve criminal justice.
- Evaluate the effectiveness of criminal justice programs and identify programs that promise to be successful if continued or repeated.
- Recommend actions that can be taken by Federal, State, and local governments as well as by private organizations to improve criminal justice.
- Carry out research on criminal behavior.
- Develop new methods of crime prevention and reduction of crime and delinquency.

In recent years, NIJ has greatly expanded its initiatives, the result of the Violent Crime Control and Law Enforcement Act of 1994 (the Crime Act), partnerships with other Federal agencies and private foundations, advances in technology, and a new international focus. Some examples of these new initiatives:

- New research and evaluation are exploring key issues in community policing, violence against women, sentencing reforms, and specialized courts such as drug courts.
- Dual-use technologies are being developed to support national defense and local law enforcement needs.
- The causes, treatment, and prevention of violence against women and violence within the family are being investigated in cooperation with several agencies of the U.S. Department of Health and Human Services.
- NIJ's links with the international community are being strengthened through membership in the United Nations network of criminological institutes; participation in developing the U.N. Criminal Justice Information Network; initiation of UNOJUST (U.N. Online Justice Clearinghouse), which electronically links the institutes to the U.N. network; and establishment of an NIJ International Center.
- The NIJ-administered criminal justice information clearinghouse, the world's largest, has improved its online capability.
- The Institute's Drug Use Forecasting (DUF) program has been expanded and enhanced. Renamed ADAM (Arrestee Drug Abuse Monitoring), the program will increase the number of drug-testing sites, and its role as a "platform" for studying drug-related crime will grow.
- NIJ's new Crime Mapping Research Center will provide training in computer mapping technology, collect and archive geocoded crime data, and develop analytic software.
- The Institute's program of intramural research has been expanded and enhanced.

The Institute Director, who is appointed by the President and confirmed by the Senate, establishes the Institute's objectives, guided by the priorities of the Office of Justice Programs, the Department of Justice, and the needs of the criminal justice field. The Institute actively solicits the views of criminal justice professionals and researchers in the continuing search for answers that inform public policymaking in crime and justice.

www.ingramcontent.com/pod-product-compliance
Lightning Source LLC
Chambersburg PA
CBHW081733170526
45167CB00009B/3800